Rosemary

[signature]

The Houses of Lympstone

Cruck truss in Hayes Raleigh

17th century leaded window at Sowden House

THE HOUSES OF LYMPSTONE

Rosemary Smith

with photographs by
Harland Walshaw

Foreword by Peter Beacham

Lympstone Historic Houses Group

LYMPSTONE HISTORIC HOUSES GROUP

First published 2011

ISBN 978-0-9569837-0-1

Set in Garamond
Printed and bound by TJ International Ltd, Padstow, Cornwall

In memory of
Ian Angus
who loved and recorded
the buildings of Lympstone
(and was very keen on bargeboarding)

Bargeboarding at Varnes

PREFACE

This has been a long investigation, spanning some years, and has nevertheless been a very exciting project. To lay flesh on the bones of what has been since the nineteenth century called "a little fishing village", and to show it has been so much more than that, through its houses, has been very rewarding. You, too, will perhaps feel the excitement of tracking down the history, and the architecture, of a house you know – like a detective story. I have been fascinated throughout my research to find how much older many Lympstone cottages and houses are than is suggested by their appearance. I have been encouraged too by perhaps finding an early document dating them beyond doubt.

I would particularly like to urge those of you with original Indentures (old legal documents), Conveyances and written records of any sort to deposit them with the Devon Record Office. They will be professionally cared for in optimum technical conditions and put at the disposal of researchers, so that the historical picture can become more complete, and puzzles solved.

Apart from documents, I have been lucky to find old paintings and engravings which tell the story of how a house looked at a certain date. The most interesting of these have been the paintings of that 18th century travelling clergyman, the Reverend Swete, who stopped in Lympstone and painted, in romantic fashion, the Darling Rock, the Vicarage (now Hayes Raleigh), and the cottage, Hares.

Buildings are listed as being of special architectural or historic interest by the Secretary of State for Culture, on the recommendation of English Heritage. In the text, all the houses in the village that are listed have their own headings. There are 93 such structures in Lympstone. Other houses that are included are highlighted in bold type.

To err is human: my mistakes are my own. As Voltaire, that wily old cynic, said: "History is a pack of tricks we play upon the dead"! Nevertheless, I have tried to present as true a picture as possible of Lympstone through its houses, and through time, from the Middle Ages to the present day.

Rosemary Smith

CONTENTS

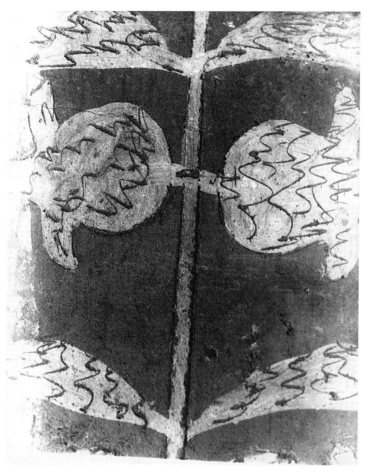

17th century sgraffito on fireplace at River Cottage

FOREWORD

Every village should have a book like this. The happy collaboration that has brought together Rosemary Smith's lively and delightfully-written history with Harland Walshaw's evocative photographs has resulted in a publication that immediately engages the imagination and stimulates the desire to walk again familiar streets and look with new eyes. These words and pictures show just how much there is to enjoy, even if we have not had the privilege of living in the houses day by day or, as visitors, persuaded an owner to allow us to poke our heads into the roof space to see a roof built four of five centuries ago.

Lympstone's houses are a microcosm of the building history of England. They represent the great social range that has typified English society across the centuries, from the architectural grandeur of Nutwell Court to the modest and charming small cottages of later centuries. They are pleasing to the eye too, not least in the way that cob and thatch comes to be admixed with later brick buildings in a satisfying harmony in the streetscene. And, of course, they span the history of building from the medieval period to our own day, with excellent examples of each period comfortably at home with each other, and with interesting examples of more contemporary styles.

This is also a very necessary book. All the legislation, all the conservation policies, all the efforts of conservation officers in the world cannot in themselves ensure the good management and sustained health of our historic buildings and places. That can only be achieved by the thoughtful stewardship of owners and managers of our heritage, almost all of it in private, not public, hands. "We are only trustees for those that come after us," William Morris famously declared in founding the Society for the Protection of Ancient Buildings in the late 19th century. This book will be of huge value in helping Lympstone to continue that trusteeship of all that makes it such a special place.

Peter Beacham
Designation Director
English Heritage
London, July 2011

ACKNOWLEDGEMENTS

I am submerged by names. This book is the result of a whole team of people, without whose efforts it would not have come to fruition. It was inspired by the seminal idea of writing the House Histories of Lympstone, proposed by Ian Angus, to whom the book is dedicated. At his suggestion, we founded the Lympstone Historic Houses Group, and though sadly he did not live to see publication, we have achieved his aims, both with the book and with the Houses Histories, which we are gradually preparing and donating to all of the ninety-three Listed Houses.

I must first thank all the members of the LHHG committee, who have done so much to help, without which it would have been impossible to write the book. Especially I would like to thank Harland Walshaw, who has been my editor, inspirer and collaborator in turns, and who has taken the photographs and designed the book; and our Chairman, Helen Dimond, for her common sense, professional expertise and helpful comments.

We have had two generous benefactors: Councillor Bernard Hughes, who was able to provide us with a grant from Devon County Council; and Simon Robshaw, who gave us a most generous and encouraging personal grant. And much of the finance has been raised by the Friends of LHHG, who have supported our events, bought our cakes, gambled on our lottery tickets, and come in numbers to our garden openings, lectures and outings, all of which have helped us to swell our coffers. And of course I am most grateful to those owners of beautiful gardens who have opened them on our behalf.

I especially want to thank all those owners who have invited me into their houses, talked about them and lent me documents, some very old, but all of great aid and interest. I am particularly grateful to Tim Dearsley of Hares for lending me twenty four Indentures about his cottage, and another three about other houses. Others who have lent me their documents include John and Catharine Hennessy of Southerleigh, Sue and Dick Waite of Sheppards, Rodney and June Dingle of Haymore Thatch, Nick Harries of Bellhangers, Mrs and Mrs Bowman of 1, Church Road, Sheila Stone of 1, Laureldale, Mrs Doreen Flowers of 1, Brook Cottages, Mrs Reece of Sowden Lodge, Robin and the late Carol Tolson of Hayes Raleigh, Jill and Clive Wilson when they owned Kilrush, David and Sue Goddard of the Mill and Nigel McCarthy of Underhill House.

I would like to thank Julie Horwood for her help in obtaining documents when she was Secretary of the Lympstone Society, and Angela

Coles, Chairman of the Lympstone History Society, for all her help and knowledge. Her columns about Old Lympstone in the Exmouth Journal are always enlightening. Without all of the above, my research would have been much curtailed.

Here I would especially like to thank Giles Body, who helped to tidy up the transcriptions I made of a great many parchment documents, adding relevant notes on abstruse terms.

The thanks continue. I am grateful to the staff of the Devon Record Office and the West Country Studies Library for all their help with documents, and to the staff of Exmouth Library for their help in research. I am indebted to Dr Todd Gray for his teaching on Local History at Exeter University, and later research on the paintings of the Revd John Swete. I also acknowledge the work of earlier local historians, the 18th century Revd Polwhele in *The History of Devonshire*, the Revd Reichel of A la Ronde, and Lympstone historians Mrs Elizabeth Scott, Mr David Burton, Mrs Rosemary Burton, Mrs Insull, wife of a former Rector, and Ralph Rochester, who has kindly helped me much with his own research. I gratefully acknowledge the work of Peter Beacham which has guided my investigations, and who has generously written the Foreword, and of Dr Cherry, whose re-survey of Lympstone houses for the 1986 Listing has underpinned many of the descriptions. I am grateful too for the inspiration of John Allan, archaeologist of Exeter Cathedral.

We are most grateful to Sue Mildenhall for designing the cover, and to Diane Tranter for creating the map.

Finally, I should like to thank the two daughters of Annie Thomas who have allowed us to quote passages from their mother's writings., which illuminate life at the Belvedere and other houses in Lympstone in the late nineteenth century. I have also used the early twentieth century memoirs of Mrs Sellars, wife of the manager of the Bakery. Brian Brockman has kindly given me access to his mother's memoirs, from which I have quoted extensively in *Chapter III*.

Here I must end for lack of space. But I do thank my family for their encouragement – and patience!

Rosemary Smith

The fanlight and panelled doorway of Exe View House

INTRODUCTION

The History of Lympstone through its Houses

Today, Lympstone appears in the landscape as an area of great beauty. The vista at the mouth of the Wotton Brook, nestling between two red breccia and sandstone cliffs, is, in certain weathers, spectacular. The eye travels over the river to faraway Powderham, the Haldon Hills and Dartmoor. Sometimes the mist comes down so low that only the red cliffs are discernible. Trees clinging to the cliff-top lour over the beach, black against the red. Hard layers of sandstone mingle with the breccia, forming strata. In the faults in the sandstone, cave mouths appear, inviting exploration, but mostly stopped up with shingle and seaweed. Cormorants perch blackly on the Darling Rock, formerly a grass-covered segment of cliff detached from the mainland, now merely a punctuation mark in the water. On a sunny day, the sparkling water, the red cliffs and the little dinghies carry the eye up the river towards the great motorway bridge spanning the Exe and on to the city and Cathedral.

Inland, the ground rises along the Brook, among fields and hedges formed by generations of farmers. Here was a stand of withies used in fishing or boat-building, there a plot of hemp, then a ploughed field of red Devon earth, there again lush pasture for cows and horses. Occasionally there is now a large field of turnips for winter feed, or yellow oil-seed rape which flames out in the landscape. Rising towards Lympstone Common, the fields grow larger, solemnly green or brown, providing feed for sheep or cattle, sometimes land for the plough. Everywhere there are copses of trees, and in the hedges, ash, hawthorn, sometimes oak, mainly two but sometimes (the earliest) up to five species. On Lympstone and Woodbury Commons, the stony and pebble-filled soil (part of the Budleigh pebble-beds, laid down some 200 million years ago), raises woods and heathlands, now maintained by professional foresters.

Lympstone and the landscape

Uniting all these territories are the little lanes, winding and often hidden within Devon banks, deep between hedges. Indeed, a feature of Lympstone is its small paths, from the often cobbled drangways round the Boat Shelter, to the unsurfaced lanes that climb over the hill separating Lympstone from Sowden, sometimes by the brook, sometimes over it. Narrow lanes continue up to the Common.

In order to understand why Lympstone houses and cottages were built as they were in different ages, we must look briefly at the landscape and environment of the village and Parish.

Lympstone is a strip parish falling from the Common at 500 feet, down to the estuary of the Exe. This has defined its character. Farms and agricultural land with their clay soils have covered the upper reaches of the parish, while lower down, there have been rich meadows and orchards along the Wotton Brook. This and its valley, and the parallel valley of Sowden, have also defined and influenced the development of the village. Both were once creeks of the river Exe, forming outlets to the estuary and sea, an opportunity for fishing, shipbuilding and trading to the outside world.

From around the Boat Shelter, and on the north side of the Brook, the village has grown by a long track laid down in Saxon times. For many years it was bordered by the 'waste' (mainly to the north side of the Strand and the beginning of Church Road), where the Lord of the Manor bred his rabbits and enjoyed his warrens. From 1175 he was also the Lord of the Manor of Woodbury, some three miles away. So far no manor house has been identified in Lympstone or Woodbury, though an old document does give a description of a manor house (then derelict) in Woodbury, where it is likely that he lived. When the Lord of the Manor of Nutwell became the Lord of Lympstone and Woodbury in 1509, there was a small village of Nutwell which housed husbandmen and fishermen, where Nutwell Court and its Lord gave protection. Nutwell village has now gone.

Building materials

What conditions produced the houses of Lympstone? If we look firstly at the geology of East Devon, we discover the materials used for building purposes. It also dictates the types of agriculture, produce and economic resources (such as quarries), indeed all life. History and economic factors influence settlement and population at different times.

From their exteriors, many of Lympstone's houses give no clue to their origins, or even the materials of which they are built. They were repaired, altered, rendered, adapted to their owners' needs, made up-to-date and fashionable according to the times (or according to their owner's pocket).

Stone

In early and medieval times, with only horse (or ox) and cart, or transport by water, men had mostly to choose what stone was available in the immediate locality. The exceptions to this were the Romans, who brought in Purbeck marble from Dorset for their forts, and the Normans, who shipped Caen stone from France for Exeter Cathedral. As roads improved and canals were built, of course, could be brought from further away: Bath stone in the eighteenth and nineteenth centuries, and Portland stone from Dorset. Chalkstone, flint, chert and New Red Sandstone, however, can all be found in East Devon.

The main stone in Lympstone itself lies on both sides of the river Exe. This is New Red Sandstone, comprising the older Triassic and the strong red Permian sandstone. Its colour ranges from red, pure white, beige, brown, green to mauve, iron oxides often staining it a deep colour. In medieval times, there was a quarry in Quarry Field by the Mill, which can still be seen. This stone was used in the 1409 re-build of the village Church, and can be seen in the tower today.

Red breccia is the other main stone available in Lympstone, and it forms the cliffs at Lympstone together with thin red strata of real sandstone. Breccia is a gravely sedimentary rock of lesser durability than sandstone, though similar. It exists on the other side of the Exe also, from Paignton up to Dawlish and Exeter.

Found near Lympstone are the Budleigh Buns or Pebble Beds, running in a line north from Budleigh Salterton, over the Common to Rockbeare and on to Bampton near the Somerset border. While they can be seen mainly as wall facings in the Budleigh area, there are only two in Lympstone. However, there are many Lympstone paths made of them: Quay Lane, paths at Fern and Hope cottages, another outside Sheppards, one by the wall of The Retreat, an area beside Town Dairy, and the path up to Rose Cottage. They are water-rounded cobbles of quartzite, a form of sandstone, now very much metamorphosed.

This geology has dictated what was used in house building here from the Middle Ages up to the seventeenth century, perhaps even further. Indeed as we look at the houses of Lympstone, we can see that they are made of three main materials - cob, stone and brick.

Cob and thatch

Although stone was used in the Middle Ages, there was a scarcity of cut stone. Men turned to what lay to hand, unbaked earth, from which they made cob, the main material for building cottages in Devon, where the clay is particularly suitable. This was used from the thirteenth century until well into the nineteenth century, and is beginning to be used again.

Cob was also the main building material of the Elizabethan age in Devon, although large houses would be built of stone. None survive in Lympstone. The pattern of sixteenth century houses here shows them established at the top end of Longmeadow Road and along the narrow lane for cattle and animals to travel to market. They occur along the village street past the church to the harbour.

Thatch covered most roofs of buildings in the medieval period, and on into the later sixteenth and seventeenth centuries. Some thatch happily still exists in Lympstone, having continued as a roofing material even into the eighteenth and nineteenth centuries. Some vestiges of very early thatch can sometimes be found, having been undisturbed but added to by thatchers. There are six dwellings we know in Lympstone which have the remains of old tree trunks supporting a thatched roof preserved beneath a Victorian (or later) slate roof.

Brick

The third building material much used in the village is brick. This did not become commonly used as a building material in Devon until the late seventeenth century, though brick is found in chimneys especially, and ovens, in the village from the late sixteenth century. This is often Dutch brick, sometimes yellow, which was imported into Lympstone and the nearby port of Topsham. This was probably brought in as ballast from ships plying to and from Holland in the serge trade There are small seventeenth century Dutch bricks in the chimney shafts of Berry Cottage, Pax Cottage, Rogues Roost, Crooks Corner and Lavender Cottage.

Possibly the first use of brick for a whole house in Lympstone was for the Queen Anne House of 1702, which was originally known as The Brick House. With the growth of brickworks (and there were many in Topsham), the use of bricks became widespread in the eighteenth century. Topsham and Lympstone were among the first to use it after the building of the Customs House in Exeter in 1680, the first known in Devon.

After the Great Fire of Lympstone in 1833, the cob and thatch cottages near the harbour were reconstructed in brick and slate. In Victorian times, the big houses, Harefield, Tedstone House and Peters Tower were built of brick, though Harefield was stuccoed. Most of the brick cottages in Lympstone are now rendered, pebble-dashed or whitewashed. Brick has been used in many cases to repair cob houses, so that they are now a mixture of materials. With building materials available from all over Devon, and even further in the nineteenth century, the same grey limestone can be seen in many of the walls around such houses as Lympstone House, The Grange and the later part of Bronte House. Brick walls are prominent too, especially in newer twentieth century building projects.

The Houses of Lympstone

In total in Lympstone there now exist 93 Listed houses, cottages, walls and limekilns. All these are listed Grade II, except the Church, which is Grade II*. Listed houses – houses of special architectural or historic importance - are protected, and consent is required for any alterations, either interior or exterior that affect the character of the building.

Mediaeval Houses

Finding common features among Lympstone's dwellings is intriguing, and these appear over and over again in a particular period. Apart from Nutwell Court, whose origins date back to the 1100s, there are nine dwellings which originated in the mediaeval period, from c. 1200-early sixteenth century. All of them have been substantially altered, but still retain evidence of their beginnings.

There was a regular pattern to these houses, with a passage from front to back, separating a service room (kitchen later) from a hall - hence their name, 'cross passage houses'. Additions such as first floors, chimneys and extensions come later, mainly from the early seventeenth century, occasionally from the late sixteenth. Cruck trusses, the curving beams supporting the roof timbers, are characteristic. In hall houses they were blackened from the smoke rising from the open hearth in the middle of the floor, as there were then no ceilings or first floor to prevent this. The smoke escaped through the thatch, or a louvre, as in Clays Cottages, Elmside and Farleys. Another important feature is the stair turret, sometimes interior, sometimes exterior, or circular stairs round a newel post. The exterior type of stair turret can be seen outside No.1 Clays Cottages, the interior type in Sowden House. These houses and cottages were all, in a small way, modelled on the much more expensive gentry hall houses.

Socially, what we are looking at in Lympstone are the houses of the more well-to-do medieval tradesmen, craftsmen, shopkeepers, small merchants and yeomen. They had houses built of more lasting materials than the draughty flimsy hovels of the labouring peasants, tied to their plot of land by the Manor. Those cottages would have lasted perhaps only one generation. As to the farmsteads, since each family had to be mainly self-supporting in food, a large area of land was needed by each to survive, and so there are some distances between the medieval farms in the village.

The Sixteenth and Seventeenth Centuries

The next group of houses to appear in Lympstone are those of the later sixteenth century. The great authority on Devon, W. G. Hoskins, has said that after the agricultural depression caused by the Black Death, by the late sixteenth and early seventeenth century there was a marked return to prosperity in Devon, with something of an agricultural boom. The recovery was fuelled by the growing demand for foodstuffs by the rising population, and by the productivity of Devonshire farming. Cromwell was to say that, "… in all the counties of England… the Devonshire husbandry is the best". In this era there came the insertion of a first floor, which could have been seen in primitive form in Berry Cottage, where it is thought a ladder led to a back loft bedroom, not over the hall. Also in this period chimneys and exterior chimney stacks, hearths and fires were fitted into more rooms than just the former hall. Chimney stacks in brick can be seen all over the village, particularly at The Sanctuary, at the Queen Anne House, at Southerleigh, Rogues Roost, and elsewhere. These developments continued during the seventeenth century.

Some of the village's seventeenth century buildings are smaller and more modest, often clusters of cottages. Outside the village itself, but still within the Parish, ('Lympstone Without' as it has been humorously put!) farms were often rebuilt, added to, or in other ways modernised. This required some capital. With prosperous tenant farmers still having the security of the three-life tenure of the Middle Ages, and with more prosperous yeomen and Lords of the Manor, modernisation was possible. Features worth noting are the continuation of the pattern of interior roofing and cruck trusses. The use of plank and muntin panelling screens across passageways (best seen at Sowden Farm), of dark long beams in the old hall, and the gradual insertion of stone or timber-framed mullion windows, is new at this time. The garde-robe or lavatory, which consisted of a seat with outside shute constructed to end some feet above the ground, as at Southerleigh, seems to have reached Lympstone in Elizabethan times. The interior fittings there have long gone, but would have included some form of seating. For houses of lesser status, people would have dug a hole in the ground outside, or carried their waste to a stream or river (here, the Brook). In the seventeenth century, also, began the import of Dutch bricks, smaller and of different colour to the English, which were much used in chimney stacks.

The Eighteenth Century
In the eighteenth century there were great changes, not only architecturally but also in economic prosperity for Lympstone. Many rich merchants, shipbuilders and owners who traded in Newfoundland, Greenland and Europe, and indeed in America (post the War of Independence) lived in Lympstone, and built themselves houses. Large houses on Burgmanns Hill

were built for renting to visitors. These properties were much influenced by London fashions and boasted classical features of pilasters and porticos, and a certain symmetry and proportion, derived from Palladianism. They had high ceilings in these big dwellings, and large windows to let in light – a great change from the previous century. Houses built in the former style hastened to put in large windows, perhaps a portico, and sometimes imitated stone coursing in the stucco finish. These houses can mainly be seen along the Strand, and again on the high ground towards the former Rectory.

In the eighteenth century, local carpenters began to put in sliding windows with the Lympstone signature of wooden stops, present in many older cottage buildings even today.

The Nineteenth Century

Nineteenth century houses are probably the most numerous in Lympstone. Cottages continued to be built of cob and thatch, but the terraces, villas and larger buildings were of brick with slate roofs, often with projecting bay windows. There are signs of unusual sophistication for a village, with occasional tuck-pointing and a carved Coade Stone doorway.[1]

The Twentieth Century

Twentieth century building tended to come in the form of housing estates. Colonel Birch's land was transformed into two roads of houses and bungalows. What was called, pre-War, 'the Unadopted' road became Greenhill Avenue, with the Police House at the end. Local Authority housing was developed above the church after the Second World War. The Ministry of Defence built an adjoining estate for the officers and men of the Royal Marines, whose Training Centre lies further down the main Exeter Road. A large private housing estate was built on the land of Underhill Farm above the Wotton Brook, and smaller groups of infilling along Strawberry Hill and Longmeadow Road. Most of these houses are of brick and slate, or incorporate concrete; bungalows of the sort found all over England, with no local character. Some are rendered or pebble-dashed.

The Twenty First Century

Finally, in the twenty first century, there are four important new houses of modern build. The Lookout is a timber-framed brick house, partially built in to the hillside, single storey with a short tower. Field House, steel framed, is a white modernist essay in concrete and glass, standing out above the Boat Shelter. Salters, by Devon architect Stan Bolt, is also of steel, concrete and glass with a block tower, dominating the Cliff on Sowden Lane. An even more recent Stan Bolt house is appropriately called Hidden House, tucked away down a drive off Courtlands Lane and hidden behind old garden walls, with only its zinc wedge-shaped top peeping above the parapet.

Having seen the common features of different periods in Lympstone, we can now much more easily peel off the layers of history within the houses. This in itself is an interesting exercise and stirs the imagination.

---

[1] Coade stone was an artificial stone of China clay, sand and crushed pre-fired material, manufactured in Lambeth from 1769 by Mrs Eleanor Coade. It was used for architectural ornaments, such as the doorways with heads in the keystones in Southernhay, Exeter.

Chapter I

LAYERING THE PAST: from the Common to the A376

As you come down from what is known as the Panhandle of Lympstone at its furthest point on the Common, you can see dwellings beginning some way below the pebble bed heaths and woods, mostly early farmhouses. Many are of great interest. The best way to appreciate this country, to see the wide views of the Exe and the far hills of Haldon, even Dartmoor, and to understand Lympstone's Parish Boundary properly, is to join the ceremony of Beating the Bounds held every four years.[1]

Looking at the buildings now, one would never guess that under their rendered plain exteriors lie centuries of age, as it were in accumulated veils. Among the first you reach is **Backenhayes Farm** on the Hulham Road, called Backynghay in an Assize Roll of 1356. Quite recently it was the abattoir for the district: now it is partially a livery for horses. Nearby is **Goodmores Farm**, also mediaeval.

Exe View House

9

Exe View House

Far back from the lane, behind a lodge and long drive, lies this typical Devon farmhouse. It was much modernised in the twentieth century, but dates back to at least the eighteenth, and was re-modelled in about 1820. It became part of the Peters Estate after 1830, together with other farms. It was tenanted for most of the time after this, notably by Brigadier and Lady Edith Brooke, who both hunted, she riding side-saddle.[2]

Exe View House is built of cob and thatch (in its early part) and there is some wattle and daub in rooms upstairs. The windows contain some old thin glass (probably eighteenth century). The early part of the house lies at the front by the pillared porch, which is in Regency style. The stables and tack rooms have a central courtyard, with an old well and barns. A new eco-barn has been built of straw bales.

Lower Coombe Farm

Tucked away in a world of its own, in a secret wooded valley behind Harefield House, lies Lower Coombe Farm, first mentioned in 1219 in an Assize Roll as the home of Godwin de Cumbe. It stretches picturesquely

Lower Coombe Farm in its valley

Bee boles in the wall of Lower Coombe Farm

along the valley bottom, the farm buildings clustered around each end. In its early parts, the farmhouse is medieval, and built of roughcast cob on stone footings. Smoke blackened beams tell of a hall originally open to the rafters, although this has long since been filled in with smaller rooms.[3] The cross-beam is typical of medieval roof construction, and there are two cruck joints, some parts of which appear to have been altered. Below, a large cruck with pegs stands at the end of the inner room.

A rare survival in a cob wall to the house are two bee-boles, with arched tops, intended for small bee skeps.[4] Their shape indicates a mediaeval date.

Lower Coombe Farm once had peat barns and a pound house, and also a cider press worked by horses. The farm lies on an old narrow green lane going towards Exe View Road, emerging opposite the drive of Exe View House.

Harefield House

Presiding over the village, high up towards the Common, stands Harefield House, a grand, cream stucco building, in what Colvin describes as "a crude Soanian style".[5] Its parapet has balustrades over the side bays, and Greek key motifs, as have the pilasters at the entrance. The two ends of the façade are supported by slightly projecting paired pilasters.   But it has long

Harefield House

since lost its main feature, a great pillared portico.   It was designed in 1830 by William Burgess of Exeter,[6] not to be confused with the High Victorian Gothic architect of Knightshayes, Tiverton and Castell Koch outside Cardiff, William Burges. He never designed with such classical restraint.

W. H. Peters, whose father had made a fortune in trade in Liverpool, had Harefield House settled on him, and he lived there from 1840 on his marriage to Mary Jane Levy. It is in her memory that the clock tower overlooking the estuary was built, and Harefield Cottages beside it, "to commemorate her kindness and sympathy to the poor of Lympstone". The history of the Peters family can be read in the tablets and stained glass windows of the parish church – a JP, a Major-General in the Hussars, an Admiral. They continued their patronage of the village, the Admiral being a founder of the Sailing Club and his wife of the Women's Institute, before the family finally left Lympstone in the 1950s. After a brief reincarnation as a Country Club, the house became St Peter's prep school for boys.

A little above Harefield lies the Victorian **Tedstone House**, built by Major-General Dowell for his retirement. General Dowell was a friend of Admiral Peters, who is believed to have given him the land.   It is now converted into flats. The views from here are splendid.

Middlecoombe Cottage

Down a little green lane just beyond Harefield, in rolling farmland towards the Common, lies Middlecoombe Cotttage, a central service room house, which is rare in Devon.[7] Detached and alone, it sits idyllically in a valley with a stream running through, a copse in front, and a grazing hillside behind. It is an eighteenth century cob and thatch cottage with a hipped roof, its façade notable for its 18-pane Lympstone lights (with wooden sill pegs) on the first floor. There are nineteenth century casement windows below. The brick extension has a steeply-sweeping corrugated iron roof, adding a sense of drama. Recent archaeological research has revealed that it was a farmhouse with outbuildings. Opposite stands a low old wall of Budleigh pobbles.

Coming down the Wotton valley,[8] we arrive at an area called Wotton hamlet in medieval times, described by the Revd. Richard Polwhele, the antiquarian and historian of Devon in 1791, who said that the main livelihood lay "chiefly in fishing", but also in lace-making.

Amongst other houses here is **Wellsacre**, with at least two wells in the grounds. Called Wellacre in the nineteenth century, it was later known as Rogues Roost, alluding to its part in the smuggling trade, which had been active in Lympstone from the sixteenth century onwards. There was a smuggler's run from Sowden End up to Sowden Farm barns, and on up Wotton Lane to a large chasm in the brook near Rogues Roost. Goods then went up towards Lympstone Common[9] and on to East Budleigh, where one of the Vicars was known to be involved, organizing the villagers as smugglers and having several secret rooms and passages in Vicars Mead, the old Vicarage. In 1783 it was estimated that the Government lost at least £2 million per annum as a result of smuggling, a colossal sum then.[10]

From 1928 Wellsacre was owned by Mollie McReddie, a great character who bred Scotties and enlarged the house, which has since been extended by its present owners. Originally, two cottages were marked on maps, and the foundations of the second cottage have been unearthed during work on the extension.

Bronte House

Sitting above the road to Exmouth, surrounded by trees, is a large white building, which is actually two houses, back to back. The older faces south, with a most attractive façade, boasting a delicate wisteria-covered verandah.

The south-facing façade of Bronte House

The roof timbers of Bronte House

This house dates from the late sixteenth century, and contains a great treasure, an early timber roof made of tree trunks, with the remains of an old thatch roof *in situ*, and a nineteenth century slate roof over the top.[11] Inside there are pretty plaster cornices.

  Some local historians think that this was the house where Nelson came to recuperate from his wounds, with his wife Fanny, after a battle in the West Indies in 1788.[12] The name Bronte House, it is said, commemorates this visit, for Nelson had been given the title Duke of Bronte by grateful Neapolitans. The house built onto the back of it was added in around 1836.[13]

---

[1] This begins with the arrival of a boat at Parsonage Style, and continues, marking the parish boundaries. Ceremonies of Beating the Bounds may be derived from Ambervalia, an ancient Roman festival to drive away the cold weather of winter, which involves people beating boundary stones or posts with sticks (formerly using boys to "bump" them). Traditionally organised by Parish Churches, it is

now often run by Parish Councils – but in Lympstone by a member of the parish. Waning in the nineteenth century, the ceremony now has an increased following.

2 Brigadier Brooke's brother's wife founded the Brooke Charity for donkeys and horses in the Middle East. The charity is now world-wide.

3 The blackened beams are in the roof over the bathroom; the cross beam has been heightened to enable people to get into the bath; and the inserted floor has been lowered. The cruck joints in this room have also been altered.

4 An old form of hive, made of straw or basket. A nineteenth century photograph shows six more bee boles in a cob wall that was removed and replaced with brick.

5 Howard Colvin, *'A Biographical Dictionary of British Architects, 1600-1840'*. Sir John Soane (1753-1837) was the great neo-classical architect, whose finest works include the Bank of England and Dulwich Picture Gallery. His own house in Lincoln's Inn Fields is now an atmospheric museum, just as he left it, a complex series of interiors stuffed full of his collection of classical objects and Hogarth's *Rake's Progress*.

6 Two of his most significant buildings in Exeter, St Showell's Church and the Public Rooms, were destroyed in the bombing of the city in the Second World War. He also built the Rectories at Cullompton and Meeth, both of which survive.

7 The entrance opens into a lobby, with a room on either side, and a kitchen behind. These are quite common in Dorset, but only four are known in Devon.

8 Called 'Wottone' in a Lay Subsidy Roll of 1330.

9 Bee Cottage, near the junction of the present road to Budleigh Salterton and Woodbury, was where smugglers sometimes went to transfer their goods to a cart covered in worzel mangels before the onward journey. It has since burned down.

10 See M. M. Oppenheim 'The Maritime History of Devon': "Much of Devon seamanship in the 18th century was exercised in the practice of smuggling, which, whatever its moral aspect, turned out first-class seamen."

11 There are six such houses with slate roofs over earlier tree-trunk and thatch roofs in Lympstone.

12 Peter Warwick of the 1812 Society supports this view. Other historians do not.

13 According to a map of 1890, Bronte House land included not only a fruit garden and kitchen garden, but a tennis court as well. A Conveyance shows that by the 1930s a house had been built on the tennis court and a bungalow on the fruit garden.

Chapter II

From Longbrook Road to Strawberry Hill

The Saddlers Arms is a nineteenth century roadside inn, standing at the turning into Lympstone. The car park was once a cattle market, where farmers gathered for auction. At that time a Magistrate described "two of the public houses in this village as practising greater irregularities than anywhere else in the neighbourhood". As a result the landlords pledged to break up their skittle grounds.

      The main artery of the village was a long winding path in Saxon times, Lympstone being a Saxon manor whose Lord, Saeward, was thrown out by the Normans. We see a great mix in dates of houses along this road. At the top end, opposite the pub, is Vine Cottage to the north, and across the road a house which was a laundry in the nineteenth century. Next to this is **Olga Terrace**, a Victorian row of bay-windowed houses, where many of those who worked on Harefield and other estates lived.

Vine Cottage

Vine Cottage, on the corner of the main road and the village street, is much older, dating from the late sixteenth or early seventeenth century. It is thatched, with the lintels of the casement windows on the first floor being at the level of the eaves. There are eighteenth century metal struts supporting the guttering, as seen in other houses of this period. Of typical stone footings and plastered cob, it has three rooms, the service end to the left of the passage. Many present beams look later, possibly nineteenth century, and the house has been considerably altered. There are A-framed trusses in the bedroom above the former hall, now the sitting room, which has an inserted brick stack. There are no smoke-blackened beams in the attic. It was almost certainly a farmstead, and shared a communal courtyard with Crooks Corner *(see Chapter X)*. What appears to have been an old stable with an upper hayloft has been extended into the courtyard behind and converted to residential use. It used to look out at a winding lane or cart track, now the A376. This track is shown in a mid-nineteenth century photograph, recording the large bend round Bronte House and the narrow lane leading on to Topsham port and markets.

Pax Cottage and Bakers Cottages

Next on the south side of the road, we come to Pax Cottage, the first of Bakers Cottages. Pax Cottage and nos. 2 and 3 were built in the early seventeenth century – until recently, Pax possessed a date-stone of 1624. Some of Bakers Cottages, built of roughcast cob on stone footings, have small old Dutch bricks in the chimney stacks, brought in to Lympstone and Topsham as ballast in ships from Holland during the wool trade. They are yellowish in colour, and only Pax and no. 3 have them intact. Sadly, occupiers and owners often did not know of their special significance and they were destroyed during repairs. The 1986 List description talks of corrugated iron roofs to nos. 4 and 5, whereas they had originally all been of thatch. (no. 8 still has the interior roof framework for a thatched cottage.) By 2008, nos. 4 and 5 had slate roofs, and now Pax Cottage is the only one to retain its thatch.

In the 1960s, Sir John and Lady Austen bought Pax Cottage, and it was they who named it. Lady Austen kept urging Sir John to buy it, which he initially refused to do, with consequent disagreements. When he finally gave in, it was to keep the peace – and Pax Cottage it became. After them, Dr. Seward, a very kindly and distinguished physician, lived here in his later years. He used to converse in Latin with one of his friends from St. Luke's College in the sitting room. Most of the other cottages date from 1840, and again there has been much alteration, especially to the windows.[1] These cottages seem to have been known as Pigs Cottages in the late nineteenth/early twentieth century as the owners kept the animals to supplement their diet and help their finances.

Further along from Bakers Cottages towards Lympstone, there is a courtyard opening, with modern houses and a repaired linhay. This was the coal yard of Noah Foxwell, coal merchant and grocer, whose delivery bicycle can occasionally still be seen around the village (but not ridden by Noah). The linhay (Devon word for open stalls for cattle and hay) has been repaired in stone. There are adjoining cottages of Victorian and more modern date. Most have the Wotton Brook at the bottom of their garden. In 1960 the brook burst its banks and flooded the houses, bursting out of the front doors onto the road to a great depth.

Longbrook Lane runs south off Longmeadow Road. Early twentieth century terrace houses have been built here, West View Terrace. Longmeadow Cottage, on the other side of the lane, is older. The lane crosses the Wotton Brook, being the old path to the Mill for centuries.

On the north side, we come to mixed Victorian terrace houses and modern bungalows before the cul-de-sac, **Malt Field**, on land behind Crooks Corner. This has recently been developed as assorted 'executive' homes.[2]

Berry Cottage, with Dutch bricks in its chimney

Berry Cottage

There is thick ancient wisteria covering the front of the thatched Berry Cottage, surely one of the most attractive houses in Lympstone. The curved cob is buttressed in parts. Poking out of the wisteria is a chimney made of small, yellowish Dutch bricks. The front garden wall is of Budleigh pebbles, or 'pobbles', rarely seen in Lympstone and only on very old houses. Originally a farmhouse, the cottage was built in the late sixteenth or early seventeenth century. It had three rooms, and the kitchen or service end was on the left of the passage. Dr. Cherry, in his listings survey, thought that ceilings were not put over the hall at first, but only over the inner room with a ladder up to the small bedroom platform. Later in the seventeenth century, first floors went in and the cottage was re-thatched, because of a fire. Also in that century another smaller room was added, used later to house cattle. In the passage between this and the kitchen is a wattle and daub wall. There was a well outside the back door, now sealed off with an iron cover. A rear sliding window replaced a much smaller one, and French and other windows were put in during the twentieth century before Berry Cottage was listed. There are many old beams in the cottage, but its greatest treasure is the   screen with muntins which divides the entrance passage from the sitting room. There is a hiding hole for coins above eye-level in the passage. At the rear of the cottage are barns where pigs were kept, and stalls for other animals.

More small cottages follow, mostly early nineteenth century, and then **Meadow Close**, a late twentieth century cul-de-sac. After this comes **South Terrace**, a Victorian development, and then an important house of early seventeenth century construction.

Rogues Roost

The name is recent, having been brought here by the previous owner from a house in Wotton Lane. Before then it was called Upcott, the ancient name of a family who lived all over Devon.[3] In 1838, a Directory records an Upcot, watchmaker, living at this cottage. Thatched up until 1960/61, it was then re-roofed in red pantiles. It is built of cob, and was of three rooms with a cross passage, the inner room being at the higher end. Small local sliding pegged windows give character to the façade. As it was a farmhouse, it had a good deal of land at the back, with an orchard. The kitchen has been added. There are cross ceiling beams in the inner room and the hall. The cottage has recently undergone some transformation, with a new kitchen extension built and extra bedrooms.

Rogues Roost

It was once the home of three Miss Howards and their brother, Adam, who lived in the converted barn next door (now **Adams Cottage**) in the early twentieth century. Miss Mary Howard was the chronicler or local historian of the village. She wrote 'Miss Howard's Notes on Lympstone' for the Parish Magazine.

After a few more modern houses and a cul-de-sac, Harefield Drive, we come to **Brook Cottage**. Originally a farmhouse, in the eighteenth century, it became a cottage with lodgings, and then a 'Lady's Academy', or 'School for Young Ladies', run by Mr. Fidler and his wife, who had seven daughters. The advertisement for the Academy specified: "Special Attention paid to Morals, Health and Manners. Ladies under ten, £22.00 per annum, Ladies over ten, £26 per annum."[4]

Elmside, Bass's Orchard & Lavender Cottage

Now we come to a splendid group of cottages on the south side of the S-bend, popularly known as 'Pretty Corner' (unheard of a generation ago).[5] These cottages are a group of three, Elmside and Bass's Orchard being early sixteenth century, and Lavender with a later addition in the same century. All are thatched, and present a picture of what Lympstone must have looked like up to the early twentieth century. There are paintings

'Pretty Corner'

and sketches showing these picturesque cottages with their black beams and whitewash dominating the corner.

The first two cottages were one, with a hall and a very primitive roof construction. The ridge is one huge long piece, supported at each end by large upright posts, possibly extending to the ground. In the middle is a jointed cruck, whose apexes are morticed and pegged. Originally there was an open hall hearth and no first floor, and so the roof timbers are smoke-blackened. The buildings are rendered, which makes different periods of construction and repair difficult to observe. The façade has a rich display of eighteenth century windows, twelve in all, of which nine are horizontal sliding windows with Lympstone wooden sill pegs. There are external rear chimney stacks to Elmside and Bass's Orchard, with tall brick shafts. Chamfered large dark beams in Elmside include pegged beams upstairs and A-frame trusses in the roof. There is also a large rear fireplace to the hall. Along the little path to the Brook, we can see several other houses and a pair of cottages, **East View Cottages** with good Lympstone windows, some recently lost. The three other houses are Edwardian and modern.

Rose Cottage, Littlecot, Ventnor and Endsleigh

On the north side of Pretty Corner there is a group of early nineteenth century brick houses, starting with Rose Cottage. This cottage and Little Cot were built as one by William Long, yeoman, grocer, cider-maker, coal merchant, businessman and merchant in 1824/25.[6] He subsequently built two more, Ventnor and Endsleigh adjoining. His son William Joseph improved on this small empire and acquired apple orchards on both sides of the road and further houses and cottages, including **Romany Cottage** on the corner of Strawberry Hill, where a relation, Miss Langdon, ran a small school. William Joseph Long also made time to be a Churchwarden at a very important time for the Church, its rebuilding under the Revd. William H. Curtler in 1862-4. The names Long's Meadow Road and Long's Brook Lane commemorate him. There is also a practical memorial to the Longs, as Charlotte Thorn Long, Mr. William Joseph's eldest sister, left the sum of £50 in 1904 as the basis of the Long Charity, which provided coal for widows and widowers of Lympstone every year – on Guy Fawkes' Day.

Two of William Joseph Long's sisters lived in Littlecot and from their front parlour, ran the little shop, "… one of those delightful places which have so sadly disappeared – where you could buy anything from a pin to a pianoforte and which smelled fascinatingly of cinnamon, saffron, strong cheese and humbugs. They also made Honiton lace to eke out their tiny living." This is from an article in the Exmouth Journal by Anne

Walsingham who describes the cottages well. "The paths of Rose Cottage and the three adjoining, were cobbled with stones laboriously selected and brought all the way from Budleigh Salterton by horse and cart … From the apples he grew, he made his own cider and the cider pound was on the site of Grange View, the home of Miss M. Apsley, and Brendon, the house of Mrs. L. B. Williams, almost opposite St. Boniface Roman Catholic Church.[7] The cider, when cased, was kept in the barn beside Rose Cottage, which in 1961 was then the home and studio of the local artist, Mr. Frank Middleditch …"

At the present day, only the pebbled path to Rose Cottage survives, with 1861, the date of its laying (but not the building of the house), picked out in deep slate-blue stones.

The gable of Ventnor, which faces west up Longmeadow Road, is one of the sights of Lympstone. Built of stone, it has red brick forked flues reaching a point at the top where they meet the chimney stack. There is a small round-headed window between the flues. Bold black lettering proudly proclaims TAYLOR MILITARY OUTFITTER[8] – just another of the many shops that Lympstone once boasted.

All four cottages are built in brick with Flemish bond, and are of a one-room plan (now with additions). There are two sliding windows with

The gable end of Ventnor

23

pegs in Rose Cottage and Little Cot, and also in the other two cottages. Original features include the fireplace in the sitting room of Rose Cottage, the door from the back of the dining room to Little Cot, and an old doorway leading to what was then the dairy.

After Ventnor, two bungalows replace the Catholic Church.[9] Further on, an overlarge recent house hides behind blank wooden fencing. **Abbotsford**, on the opposite side, has spacious Victorian rooms and a large garden, running down by the side of Stone Lane. We reach Romany Cottage and Strawberry Hill on the north, and the lane to the Mill on the south.

---

[1] What has been lost are some of the sliding windows with unique Lympstone small wooden sill pegs, made by a local Lympstone carpenter c.1780-1820, according to the late Tim Tapscott.

[2] On the Longbrook Lane side up to Pretty Corner, formerly Brook Corner, there were green meadows, called 'Frogs' Meadows'. Opposite Longbrook Lane there was once a blacksmith's shop. The last occupier was a George Setter, who left to work as its blacksmith at Dartmoor Prison.

[3] An Upcott was a lawyer for the Bonvilles of Shute, murdered by a Courtenay gang in the Middle Ages.

[4] In the nineteenth century, William Joseph Long of Rose Cottage dug a culvert with a barrel tunnel for the stream that came down from the fields behind Brook Cottage and over the road "helped by a Mr. Whitcher of Brook Cottage". This arched and ceiled culvert has been investigated recently and found to be in excellent condition.

[5] It used to be called Brook Corner.

[6] This date is verified by an Indenture allowing him to build on Manor land provided it was completed in a few months.

[7] St Boniface, designed in 1956 by Joseph E. Walter and built in red sandstone. Demolished in 2000.

[8] This shop probably opened in World War I, with so many soldiers billeted here.

[9] Further on from the two bungalows, the houses Byfield, Applecombe and Paddocks were built in 1955 by Snow and Yeo, on ground originally owned by the Grange. It appears this ground was used during World War I for huts to billet soldiers, and large quantities of road stone can still be found about 8 inches below the surface of the present gardens.

Chapter III

From Strawberry Hill to Sheppards Lane

We have now reached Strawberry Hill, which rises towards the Dissenters' Meeting House on Meeting Lane. At the bottom begins Church Road. **Aggie's Orchard**, a relatively new bungalow, has a large orchard going down to the Brook, full of well-kept fruit trees. In spring, the blossom there is enchanting. Next is an old cottage, once thatched, now with red pantiles, which has a long history.

Hares

Hares turns its back on the road, and faces south. In spite of the plain exterior, and with its newly-built annexe and uniform-coloured render, it is clearly an old house. We know that from 1695 the cottage had been part of the Manor,[1] until it was sold off to its tenants in 1722 (like much Lympstone property that year) to pay off the drink and gambling debts left by Sir Thomas Putt of Gittisham, Lympstone's Lord of the Manor. Twenty-three original documents, which take us back to the seventeenth century, throw much light on the concern with property among the more well-to-do tradesmen, mariners, small merchants and yeomen of Lympstone at the time.[2] It was acquired by Thomas Hare, a carpenter and joiner, who paid off a debt of £124 to establish his claim in 1726, and it remained in that family for 140 years. When one of the members died instate in 1831, the Archbishop of Canterbury had to appoint his son as Administrator. It remained in the Hare family until 1898.[3]

Hares seen in a nineteenth century watercolour

The cottage, which probably dates from the mid-late seventeenth century, is mainly constructed of cob and stone - the right hand side, with its wide entrance arch built of brick, is a later addition.[4] Inside is an attractive inglenook fireplace and a late screens passage with panels of differing designs. There is good oak panelling in the garden-facing entrance hall and in the dining room. Once again, there is a (later) horizontally sliding window with Lympstone wooden sill pegs to the first floor. A-trusses feature in the bedroom over the stable entrance on the road. This part of Church Road was known as Pigs Lane in the nineteenth century, no doubt because all smallholders and agricultural workers kept pigs to enliven their diet and keep down costs.

1 & 2, Laureldale

This is an elegant pair of brick houses, which look as though they have been plucked from a Regency seaside resort and dropped into Lympstone. Sandwiched between much earlier cob cottages, they are bow-fronted on both storeys, one bay each, with semi-circular barred fanlights over the doors. The dark red brick is laid in Flemish bond, and is tuck-pointed to give an air of sophistication. This continues into the particularly fine early nineteenth century panelled interiors, quite unspoilt, with a pretty

No 1, Laureldale

Panelling in 1, Laureldale

plasterwork cornice in the front room. The bows have an inside curved wooden shutter that slides up and down, an unusual and outstanding feature. It is said that these houses were built, in the early nineteenth century, to let to "Ladies from London", and they certainly do not feel like houses for villagers. They are as smart and fashionable as any in Lympstone.

Haymore Thatch and Town Dairy Cottage

Two thatched cottages, a pleasure to see, were one cottage in the eighteenth century. They are of two storeys, and stand forward of the infill line of the Laureldales on the road, as befits an earlier resident. While their front one-room wings are built of cob, blocked and plastered on stone footings, the rear gables are of brick with slate roofs and of the nineteenth century. They have small first floor windows, with their lintels at eaves level. Haymore Thatch has a beautiful window that turns the corner round a circular bar, formerly a shop window for the dairy, which sold milk, cream and greengrocery. The bracketed fascia board above the window is decorated with a pattern of holes.

The house becomes more alive when we know that John Moore, dairyman, lived at Haymore Thatch in 1878, according to the Harrod's Royal Directory of that year. The house has old interior beams in a room

Haymore Thatch and Town Dairy Cottage

which possibly was the old entrance. There is a meat store with hooks for hanging hams, now a bathroom. A-frame beams are found in the bedroom above the old shop. Downstairs we see steps down to what was once the old dairy, where the cream was made, and where there used to be a big iron range when this room was the kitchen. Many in the village can still remember cows coming every day down the road to the farm to be milked.

Beyond this, on the south side, is a small green lane, which leads towards the Mill and Meadowgate. Tucked in behind Town Dairy Cottage is an old farmhouse on the side of the lane, built of cob, and with chamfered beams in the back and hall. Two separate roofs have been found, the lower one with tree trunks for beams, and so possibly of the late seventeenth century. The second roof above is of ordinary timber.[5]

On the north side of Longmeadow Road, after Strawberry Hill, there are a number of great trees which form quite a landmark, and a (newly rebuilt) stone wall, part of the garden of Lympstone House *(see Chapter X)*. The wall turns the corner to the church, and ends in gate piers and a **lodge** . This was the entrance to the drive up to Lympstone House, but now only goes as far as **The Retreat**, once the stables of the larger house, which was turned into a dwelling in the 1930s. The curved arches of the façade, now filled in, suggest its origins. A cottage in the lee of the chancel of the Church, **Glenhaven**, was part of the Glebe in the eighteenth century as Hayman's Tenement, and was assessed by the Revd. Gidoin in the late eighteenth century at £800, the second most expensive in the Glebe. It has a signature scratched on an upstairs window-pane, "… Hayman". A Mrs. Dowling remembers her grandmother saying the cottage had been a Lending Library at one time.[6]

Then comes the red stone **Parish Church**, which stands magnificently on one of the most important sites in the village. It was first documented in 1228, but what we see now is a Victorian building, by Edward Ashworth, with a tower built in 1409. Opposite are green meadows.[7] A recent archaeological dig yielded evidence of a large house once standing on this site.

A hill runs up past the west front of the mediaeval church tower, with **the school** at the top, a red brick Victorian building erected in the 1870s after the Forster Education Act made schooling compulsory for all children. The main windows are pointed lancets, in homage to the fifteenth century Gothic of the church across the road. A charming little wooden **Church Hall** lies just below it, an archetypal village building, and at the top of the hill stands the 1930s brick **Village Hall**.

Houses on the south side of Church Road resume with an Edwardian house of patterned brick called **The Firs** (though none can now be seen!). It was built by the miller, William Linscott, for his retirement in 1902, when he handed the running of the Mill over to his nephew, Edwin. The house faces the field rather than the road, so that the Mill is visible from its windows.

The terraces of eighteenth century cottages that continue on either side of the road form an attractive group with the church, Lympstone's finest piece of villagescape. We start on the south side of Church Road.

1, Church Road[8], Bellhangers[9], Dingles

White-rendered, with thatch on one of the three, these seventeenth century cottages (with later alterations) form a beautiful group. No. 1 has a particularly attractive bow window below, and an oriel above. Dingles retains its thatch, and has a shop bay window.

There is architectural evidence that the first two were originally built as a single structure of earth-plastered timber studwork and lath, finished in lime plaster. The front door was probably that of the present no. 1. Both were thatched, as is seen in a photograph of 1904, but now have slate roofs.[10] The floorboards in the attic remain, and are very wide, possibly seventeenth or eighteenth century. No. 1 was converted into a shop in the nineteenth century, when it acquired its bow window. There is a 'winder' (a staircase climbing behind the chimney), an early feature.

1, Church Road, Bellhangers, Dingles, Oak Cottage

Bellhangers has a sliding sash window to the right of the front door. Elm tree trunks form the A-frame beams in the roof on the third floor, still with their bark and adze marks in the wood. The staircase again is a winder, and downstairs there is an old cupboard with butterfly hinges of the early eighteenth century. There is another horizontal sliding window (with wooden pegs) to the rear of the living room.

Dingles seems to have been a shop from the eighteenth century until late in the twentieth. In the 1750s it was owned by a Woodbury oyster farmer,[11] and then it was a bakery, which it remained for at least 100 years. It later became a grocers and sweet shop.[12]

Oak Cottage

Oak Cottage, which is attached to Dingles, is mostly of the nineteenth century, with perhaps some seventeenth century fabric. The front is asymmetrical, with only two ground floor windows in the wall to the street, one of them a hornless sash, one a recent casement, with two sash windows above. The slate roof has wavy bargeboards at the end gable. The tall brick chimney stacks are monuments to the thatched roof which they once soared above, to keep the sparks off the thatch. An extension behind is mid-twentieth century. Like many of the houses on this side of Church Road, it has a long garden going down nearly to the Brook (then much deeper and wider). Formerly this steep slope supported some old ship building yards with mud berths, and the finished boats were floated down to the river on the full tide.

On the north side of Church Road, after the church, the buildings begin with **Church Cottage**, a nineteenth century house which wasn't there in the Spreat lithograph of 1842,[13] which shows Glebe cottages on the site. They were demolished to enlarge the graveyard.

The Forge, Smeaths and Alwyne

This is an attractive terrace of eighteenth century thatched cottages, with eyebrow dormer windows in the thatch, giving third floor attic rooms. A nineteenth century photograph shows a longer terrace, stretching almost to Church Cottage, but half was destroyed in a fire. As a result, the first of the cottages, The Forge, has a cobbled courtyard, enclosed by double gates and the former forge which gives it its name. The middle cottage, Smeaths,[14] has a shallow bow rising through its two storeys with hornless sash windows, and Alwyne a ground floor canted bay window. These two have moulded door frames and small rectangular fanlights. They are built of rendered cob on stone footings, though The Forge was almost completely reconstructed in the 1970s, and has a brick end wall.

Opposite, on the south side of Church Road again, beyond Oak Cottage, there's a small nineteenth century house, **Briar Cottage**, next to the even smaller **Holly Cottage**, whose roof timbers date it back to the seventeenth century. It contains another 'winder' stair behind the chimney breast of its inglenook fireplace. It is said that Florence Nightingale spent holidays in Holly Cottage as a child.

Havering, Eleanors, Sheppards

The gable end of Havering, which faces you as you walk down Church Road, is of greater interest than the plainer frontage. Rising above a modern lean-to conservatory are a canted oriel window with a 16-pane hornless sash beside it, and a round-headed window with two pointed lights above. The whole composition is surmounted with wavy bargeboarding. The façade is of two bays, and the doorway has pilasters and a moulded cornice, with a rectangular fanlight. This nineteenth century house of plastered brick is the end of a terrace of three.

The first of these three adjoining houses to be built was the middle one, Eleanors, which dates from Sarah Moreing's tenement in the eighteenth century. The façade has elegant sash windows with shutters, and the door frame has panelling,   a moulded canopy,   and a geometrical

The circular staircase at Sheppards

fanlight. Its older name was Moreens (presumably a corruption of Moreing), but during redecoration some years ago, the inscription 'Cowd's, Drapers' was found over the lintel. The Cowds were a family of tailors and drapers, who owned all three houses in the 1870s, and must have at some time used Eleanors as a shop.

There is an evocative description of life in the house by Mrs Enid Brockman, the daughter of the schoolmaster Samuel Sheppard,[15] who lived there from the 1880s, when it was called Moreens: "All the time we lived at Moreens we used a Hip Bath, in front of the kitchen fire. We had oil lamps and candles – no gas or electric stoves, but the kitchen had a big black iron stove, which had the fire on one side and the oven the other side… Of course coal was cheap then so we got good fires."[16]

The Sheppards bought the next door house, which is now named after them. The brickwork is tuck-pointed, for greater elegance. At some point the Cowds had inserted a bay shop window. The front door surround is a striking feature in carved Coade stone, as Enid Brockman described: "We had a lovely front door, the sides were long panel strips of bunches of grapes, always well painted." She does not mention the beautifully wrought circular staircase in Sheppard's, one of the handful of outstanding staircases in Lympstone. She goes on: "At first at bottom of garden there were stables – necessary for use then. Later Dad had the stables demolished – and an open roofed Summer house put in its place. We used this a lot for sitting and picnic meals. Then he had a lawn made right across the bottom of Moreens and Fair View gardens… We all loved this lawn – a wall on two sides, shrubs the other side – plants and flowers, lovely Honeysuckle, and in one corner we had a hammock – all really charming."

---

[1] Before then it had belonged to Richard Pyke, Mariner, and after him his widow.

[2] They also take us back to the constrictions of medieval laws concerning customs, e.g. 'heriot' (payment of a large sum on a death), and 'dower', whereby a widow was entitled to 'Thirds' or yearly rent from property owned by her late husband.

[3] When one of the Hares died inestate in 1831, the administration of the property was sorted out by The Archbishop of Canterbury and Thomas Hare Hare, the Heir to the Estate.

⁴ The arch appears in a painting by the Revd. John Swete in the late eighteenth century.

⁵ Six such roofs have been found in Lympstone of similar construction, with old tree trunks for beams, with some of the old thatch still on them, and a slate roof.

⁶ Mrs. Dowling, who was a village resident, remembered correctly. At the turn of the nineteenth/twentieth century Miss Augusta Dick, daughter of General Dick of The Cottage, was the secretary to the Lending Library.

⁷ The antiquarian Richard Polwhele described it in 1791: "Directly opposite the church are some fine meadows, through which we have a pleasant rural walk to the hamlet of Sowdon. Passing under several little rustic arches we pursue a path that winds delightfully through the fields, by the side of willows, or amidst clumps of overshadowing elms. When we have reached the hamlet of Sowdon, we are charmed with its neatness, and the gardens and orchards around it. And we are happy to discover, that here are very decent lodgings for our temporary accommodation, if we chuse to explore further the beauties of this snug retreat."

⁸ A note from the late Edmund Jupp says "There are two No. 1, Church Road houses, the other at its end by Burgmann's Hill. Funny place, Lympstone!"

⁹ In the late nineteenth century, Bellhangers once housed a family concerned with fitting domestic bell systems, hence the name.

¹⁰ A fire in the 1990s destroyed the old roof, with its beams and clues to its age.

¹¹ Phillip Perriam of Woodbury farmed oysters in the estuary from Dingles. An Indenture of his was lent kindly by a previous owner. Lympstone was well-known for its Oyster beds in the eighteenth century, when "The Woodbury Salterton and Lympstone Manor Court Book" summarises a rental of "Oyster Balls at 2d Each yearly" and shows a large oyster industry in Lympstone and the Exe.

¹² In the 1970s, Albert Langmead recorded memories of his Edwardian childhood in Lympstone, when Dingles was still a bakery. It was a shop selling groceries and sweets at the time of the recording.

¹³ W. Spreat of Exeter published a book of stone lithographs of Devon churches in 1842. A copy of the Lympstone lithograph hangs in our church vestry.

[14] The whole row was called Smeaths Cottages in the nineteenth century, after Mary Smeath, who was the lessee of "three Dwellinghouses, Orchard and Garden adjoining." The Tithe Records of 1839 show there were six houses and two gardens there. An orchard rose on the site of the present School House. There was a spring in the grounds of Smeath's to which The Forge had a right of way.

[15] Samuel Sheppard was headmaster of the boys' school in Lympstone from 1880-1920, and organist at the parish church, where there is a window in his memory.

[16] We are grateful to Brian Brockman for access to his mother's memoir.

Chapter IV

From Sheppards Lane to Burgmanns Hill

The buildings along Church Road are interrupted after the Lane by long stone walls, on either side of the street. The limestone wall on the north side runs all the way from Alwyne, and was the wall of the grounds of Varnes, one of the most interesting houses in Lympstone.

Varnes

Half-hidden behind a screen of trees, an elevated Regency façade presides over Church Road, its wisteria-clad iron and glass veranda running the length of the house. The early nineteenth century casement windows have thin, elegant glazing bars, and cusped barge boarding decorates both gable ends. Now divided into two, it was originally a cob farmhouse with a thatched roof, built in the sixteenth century to a three-room through-passage plan, with a service-end rear wing. There are beautiful trees in the garden alongside, and it was once called Laburnum Cottage because of one particularly lovely specimen. Now there is a great copper beech, gracefully standing guard over the garden.

Inside are chamfered ceiling beams and cross beams, and hollow moulding to the hall. It is possible that two jointed crucks survive above the hall and passage. In the seventeenth century Varnes acquired a remarkable treasure, a sgraffito (or scratched pattern) in the rear sitting-room fireplace, with two layers of coloured plaster, black and white. While such patterns as these (diagonally halved squares) are the most common, sgraffiti have a rarity value and are relatively sparse, although a different example is to be found in Lympstone at River Cottage (*See Chapter VI*).[1] There is evidence of two earlier fireplaces behind this one, which could help to date the house. Other features from the seventeenth century are the Dutch bricks in the kitchen chimney and the upper part of the sitting room chimney. The early house was gradually extended to the rear into the hill, perhaps incorporating farm outbuildings and the dairy.

A notable owner was Richard Withall, who acquired the house from the Manor of Lympstone in 1684. The Withalls were rich merchants, and sailed their own boats on the triangular voyage from Devon to Newfoundland to the Continent via the Azores. It was in the late eighteenth century that the Rector's brother, another clergyman, John Lewis Gidoin, lived at Varnes with his mother, and it was he who had the house gentrified.

Varnes

The extension to the west was added much later by a Dr Barton who used it as his surgery. In the 1990s, the house was divided into two and much of the extensive grounds sold off. Where once there had been a tennis court and bowling green, there are now houses, including a development above called Withalls Gardens.

On the south side of Church Road after Sheppards Lane there is an ancient long wall of red sandstone, badly eroded in its lower courses by the passage of vehicles, with a later brick upper storey. Where it turns at right angles down Sheppards Lane it is all brick, enclosing Southerleigh garden, and this part collapsed just a few years ago and had to be rebuilt. The builders found old sandstone footings, which, after about ten yards, returned at a right angle. The footings enclosed a small area, which might have been a barn, or a priest's house, or the church ale house… Behind this wall is the garden of an extremely interesting house.

Southerleigh

A thick wooden cornice runs around the top of the walls of Southerleigh, the main feature of its restrained plastered façade. The sash windows with thick glazing bars are irregularly set. It is a substantial village house, probably dating from the late sixteenth century when it was surely built as a

The ancient wall and Southerleigh

farmhouse. Its original plan presents a puzzle, though it was possibly a three-room through-passage house with a rear-end service wing.

Among the many discoveries is an old fireplace in the present dining room, centred to the left, perhaps because the stairs had not then been built. There are many ceiling chamfered cross-beams, and upstairs a very old, possibly sixteenth century partition was removed in the twentieth century. Another great discovery has been the remains of an old (Elizabethan?) garde-robe (or lavatory) up the stairs to the third floor attics, with an external open shaft below. This shaft ends about three feet up from the garden underneath. It would have been used also to hang clothes (hence garde-robe) to fumigate them.

Deeds and Indentures survive describing the owners of the house back to 1774, and include many well known eighteenth century local characters, until Robert Andrew Titcher "Shopkeeper of Lympstone" (Chemist and Druggist) bought Southerleigh. By 1857 an Abstract of Title notes that *"This property is old and dilapidated…"* and was let for *"an annual rent of £30"*. It was sold to a Miss James of Okehampton, and Snips Stamps[2] recorded a story about this family:

"At Southerleigh lived some folk called James who had seven daughters. Some time after the railway came [in 1861] and there was still a dispute regarding the right of way to Exmouth, one of the James' girls was walking to Exmouth. She was stopped by a railway policeman, who said she was going to be summoned for trespassing on railway property. A summons was duly issued, but when the time came to serve it a Miss James came to the door and refused to accept the summons, saying she had never walked along the railway!"

The Redwing Inn

This pub was built of brick in the early nineteenth century, and has a double depth plan and three storeys, with a single storey extension. It is now rendered and painted. There is a wide moulded wooden cornice at ground floor level on the exterior, and beneath it tripartite sash windows, and a round-headed door.

The tale is told that its original name of The Vaults was because of the graveyard of the Unitarian Chapel, which once stood on the ground next door. The daughter of a former landlady remembers her mother being anxious that some of her (inebriated) customers, who staggered out towards the gravestones and clutched at them for support, might seriously injure themselves.

There are no gravestones or ghosts any more, just a car park and some garages before we reach **Ellenthorpe**, a tall gabled Victorian house, romantically clothed in creeper, with a long descending stretch of land, part of which was once a boatbuilder's yard, now a most beautiful garden. The Unitarian Chapel which once stood on the site was built in 1820, when Gulliford became too far for some Dissenters. It was taken over by the Wesleyans in 1850, but later demolished. The creeper extends next door, to two bijou Victorian houses, **Rose Cottage** and **Fuchsia Cottage**, built in brick.

On the north side of the road, is a group of fine houses of the late eighteeenth/early nineteenth century. The first of this group was called Wistaria when it was all one, and still has a wisteria growing up its face. It was part of a large plot of land leased by Sir Thomas Putt in 1718 to Jacob Manston, "the best Shipwright…" "…reserving unto his heirs forever all Waif Estrays Felons Goods, Felons themselves Deodands and Treasure Trove … with liberty to hunt hawk fish and fowl at all times reasonable". It is now divided in two, **Wistaria Cottage**[3] and **Piper's Folly**. Recently an old well was discovered below the floor of the right hand house, which had perhaps been part of an exterior courtyard.[4] The last we know of Wistaria is in the Second World War, when many Royal Marines and their families came up from Plymouth, posted to the camp at Lympstone. Provost Sergeant Chard's mother and some of the family found themselves in Wisteria, and delighted in the garden! The house was then all one.

Figgins

Figgins is an attractive stuccoed villa, four square with a hipped slate roof, set above the road. The front range is single depth with a room on either side of the entrance hall. It has a pretty shaped eaves fascia and diamond paned casement windows to the side (added in the 1960s). This part dates from the early nineteenth century. To the rear is an earlier wing which it is not possible to date precisely and which could have been part of a larger original property. In the nineteenth century it belonged to Francis Yarde Searle who was the collector of the Poor Law Rates for the St Thomas Union Workhouse. During recent building work a receipt book was found in the attic which features a number of well known names in Lympstone at that time: Linscott the miller, Hayman, Bass, Challis and Litton. More recently it belonged to the sculptor Ken Carter, who had a studio in the barn to the rear of the house and who is best known in Devon for the sculptures that line the walls of the Chapter House of Exeter Cathedral.

Claremont and Corner House

Two houses from the days of Jane Austen, which would grace any street. The semi-detached pair, built of brick in Flemish bond, form a symmetrical whole on a prominent corner site, standing proud above Church Road, and with the view from the hill over the lower gardens and fields down to the Brook and up the hill opposite. The symmetrical frontage is a five-window range, with the windows above the doorways blocked. The semi-circular traceried fanlights contribute to the air of elegance.

Claremont has a double depth plan, with a principal room on either side of the entrance passage, and secondary rooms behind. Inside is a second fanlight halfway down the hallway. There is much remaining delicately moulded decorative coving to the ceilings of the hall, drawing room and bedroom – angels and roses in a Regency pattern. Everywhere there are good examples of wood beading and skirting boards, original panelling in the drawing room beneath the window, shutters which have been made to work, and there are even the old servant bells in the back hall, hanging on strap wires waiting to summon the maid! One of the finest interior features of the house is the original staircase, rising to the third floor.

Figgins, Claremont and Corner House

One of the dormer windows in the slate roof of Corner House has a bowed front, another refinement. The garden behind rises steeply uphill (the side of a valley cut by the Wotton Brook many thousands of years ago) and has eighteenth century walls at the top.

---

[1] Other examples are to be found at Nutwell Court and Gulliford Farm.

[2] Snips Stamp was one of the fishermen in the 20th century, and as a boy went in every morning before school to draw water from the well for the occupants of Southerleigh, for which he earned 7d per week and his breakfast!

[3] There is still an old Fire Insurance company's sign on the wall.

[4] Two daughters of Captain Williams of Sowden House, the Misses Mary Ann and Jane Williams occupied it in 1823. They made a garden opposite between where Ellenthorpe and the garages now are (then the Unitarian Chapel), and "Mr. Fitcher's stable" on the east. Mary Ann lived there for forty years.

Chapter V

From Longbrook Lane to Highcliffe House

From the top of the village we turn south down Longbrook Lane. It follows a winding track, copying the meandering of the Mill leat. This was the old track to the Lord's Mill, which everyone was obliged to use.

As we climb the hill after the Mill fork, there is a long drive on the left up to a relatively modern house built by the farmer, Mr. Wilfrid Bailey, on ground which had been 'the pleasaunce of Sowden House', called Paradise. After a big stone wall round an old orchard, we come down to Sowden House, lime-mortared with a newly slate tiled roof with three prominent dormers (formerly thatch, then 'peggies', slates with wooden pegs to hold them). There is a porch with pillars, and the house once had railings, cut down in the second World War.[1]

Sowden House

Sowden House stretches out along the roadside, a distinguished-looking building with a classical porch, and beside it a long barn with a picturesque Gothick window. Parts were re-built around 1700, shortly before members of the Drake family from Buckland moved to Lympstone. It was later re-modelled and all its windows renewed, probably when Captain Thomas Williams, R. N., retired here from the Royal Navy in the early nineteenth century.

The two room cross passage plan, the newel stair, the exterior chimney stack, the one acre strips on either side of the house, all prove that it was a re-build of an earlier house, when Sowden was a separate manor, during the time of Lady Mary de Pomfret in the thirteenth century.[2]

The house was originally thatched (a thatching needle has recently been found under the peggies), and the façade is a nineteenth century addition – behind it is an older pink sandstone frontage, with cob above. A very big beam with adze marks was discovered when the kitchen ceiling fell down. This lies across the window near the old bread oven, and shows that the kitchen was part of the older building. The former dining room next to the kitchen has a rounded beam, both above the ceiling and below, with a squared end.[3]

That Sowden House was involved in smuggling has been a village tradition for centuries. The story goes that the smugglers had two runs – one to Parsonage Stile, the other to Sowden End. The Preventive Officers (four of whom lived in the village at one time!) were, it is presumed, enticed

Sowden House

by gifts of smuggled tobacco or brandy to go to the run where smuggling was _not_ planned. On the Sowden End run, the smugglers would come up to Sowden House, hide the goods and then take them on up the deep course of the Wotton Brook to the former Rogue's Roost (now Wellsacre). The goods would then go on up to the common, or a cottage known as Bee Cottage (now gone), hidden under mangles or other vegetables. They would be taken to East Budleigh, Otterton, or village markets elsewhere.[4] As to the story of a secret passage from Sowden House to the beach at Sowden End, many have talked of it, but none has been found.

A description of this house would not be complete without Miss Howard's notes on people living there during the Napoleonic wars, when there was great fear of Napoleon invading England. "All along the coast people were making preparations to flee inland when Bonaparte landed. An old lady living in Sowden House used to tell how they had money sewn up inside their stays and horses ready in the stables so that they might set off for Dartmoor when the warning beacons were lit!"

We now take a detour, turning left up Courtlands Lane, with its string of twentieth century houses. But down a long curving drive, hidden from view, there lies **Sowden Lodge**, in a superb position, looking down over fields to the river at a point which was once called The Bight.

Sowden Lodge

Sowden Lodge consists of a seventeenth century cottage to which a Georgian house with a classical portico has been added. There is a fine staircase in the entrance hall. From the eighteenth century it was a gentleman's house, until it was bought in 1931 by a Miss Martino, who on the outbreak of war ran it as a nursery for evacuee children, mostly from Bristol. A present day resident of Lympstone remembers coming down to the Lodge with her charges after the wartime bombing of the Wills' Tobacco family house in Clifton. Sowden Lodge itself was bombed and strafed. It was later turned into flats, but was returned to its glory as a family house some sixteen years ago.

High limestone walls once enclosed the kitchen garden, but there now peeks over the top the zinc roof of a very recent wedge-shaped house by Stan Bolt, the architect of Salters *(described later in this chapter)*. It is called **The Hidden House**, for good reason, and is designed to take advantage of the view over the estuary, with the living accommodation on the top floor, and large plate glass windows.

Further along lies Courtlands House, not strictly in Lympstone, for the border with Exmouth runs through the grounds, but as it has been part of village life, especially when Sir Garbutt Knott lived there, it seems worth including in this book.

Courtlands

The imposing house stands out white against the hill seen from the river. It was described in 1813 as "an elegant mansion encircled by thriving plantations and gravel walks, with walled kitchen gardens, melon pits and hothouses."[5] Today the elegant house is much enlarged with nineteenth century additions, and is now encircled with new houses built in its grounds, although its green acres still sweep down to the estuary.

It is a large stuccoed mansion, parts of which are probably eighteenth century or older, though much of what we see dates from the nineteenth century. It is basically a villa, quite plain except for its moulded cornice, which has been extended by later additions, including a substantial stable yard. The sides facing the view to the estuary have an attractive Victorian verandah, decorated with a scroll design. There is a massive stone porch, heavily carved with capitals and roundels. Flanking the steps opposite is a pair of upright delicately-carved stone herons, also nineteenth century. Behind is a castellated stone wall which faces out to Courtlands Lane. At the entrance to the drive is little Gothick lodge.

Charles Baring, who lived at Courtlands in the second half of the eighteenth century until his death in 1829, was buried at Gulliford, where he had paid for the building of a replacement chapel in 1774 *(see Chapter X)*. He was a wool merchant, the brother of the founder of Barings Bank,[6] and

Courtlands

the grandfather of the great folksong collector and author of the hymn *Onward Christian Soldiers*, the Rev. Sabine Baring-Gould. In the 1870s Courtlands became the retirement home of William Lethbridge,[7] co-founder of W. H. Smith with his eponymous partner.

In 1921, Sir Garbutt Knott, who had inherited a fortune from his father's shipping line, bought Courtlands. He converted the 87 acres into an up-to-date model farm, including a model piggery and cattle house. He loved his animals, and trained his Alsatians to rescue people from fires, his pigeons to settle on him, and his goldfish to rush through the pond towards him at a signal. But as regulations changed, his fine herd of Jersey cattle had to make way for arable farming and market garden produce. During the Second World War even the tennis courts were ploughed up and cabbages planted. It was Sir Garbutt who did most to make Courtlands a part of Lympstone. Films that he made show the village Flower and Vegetable Show in the grounds, and the annual school sports. He paid for the Lympstone Band's uniforms, and gave a large contribution to the rebuilding of the boat shelter in 1935, as well as personally coming to lend encouragement and direction to the village fishermen who built it. He often took them off to the pub for refreshments. It was Sir Garbutt who encouraged Stanley Long, his neighbouring farmer, to preserve his land for future generations. Stanley Long bought Courtlands' fields after Sir Garbutt's death, and in 1966 gave them and his own land of Lower Halsdon Farm to the National Trust, protecting Lympstone from being swallowed up by the encroaching development of Exmouth.

We now retrace our steps down Courtlands Lane, until we reach a turning on the left, which takes us down a small lane till we reach the drive up to **Atlantis**, a 1930s house which stands on the heights overlooking the estuary, but whose view is hidden by the impressive cluster of mature trees that surround it. The lane bends sharply, and on our right is:

Sowden Cottage

Sowden Cottage is small, charming and thatched, dating from the late seventeenth century, on a slope planted with trees and bushes. Pretty white wooden railings enclose its front garden As usual for a cottage of this period in Lympstone, it is built of roughcast cob. Presumably it was a farm cottage for Sowden Farm, opposite.

Sowden Farm

Sowden Farm lies in the valley bottom of what was once a stream running down to the river at Sowden End. Built in sandstone, and with a mellow appearance, it is one of the most atmospheric houses in Lympstone.

Plank & Muntin screen, Sowden Farm

On one side it has a farmyard with farm buildings around, on the other there is a pond. The farm looks down the valley to the railway. It dates from the early seventeenth century and has a Georgian wing. There are mullioned windows to the front, and two external chimney stacks. Inside, it is a house of great atmosphere, with its exposed beams, oak screen and great stone fireplace with its massive lintel. Its great glory is the fine plank and muntin screen, whose lower part has been replaced with wall. The house was originally a three-room, through-passage type. There is a large ceiling crossbeam in the atmospheric main room, which was extended into the former dairy. There are jointed crucks in the roof. Sowden Farm was until the twentieth century part of Nutwell Manor.

Further on, the Victorian **Southtown House** was built with stone from the other side of the river. It is a gentleman's house, with hall, morning room, drawing room and kitchen with servants' quarters. Once occupied by the Revd. William Wilberforce Howard, Inspector of Schools in 1878-1890, and then more recently by Mr. Philip Scott, a surgeon, and his wife, Elizabeth, a local historian, to whom we owe much knowledge of our village.

We continue down a narrow and winding lane, typical of Devon countryside with hedges on top of banks, making a secret passage between green fields with trees rising on either side. From there we have a view of the river and beyond, to the Haldon Hills and Powderham, and on a good day to Dartmoor. This view is seen again even better after the railway bridge, when we reach the river Exe.

On our left, overlooking the estuary, we see a newly built house tucked modestly into the hillside, though with a short tower with windows to all sides, to take advantage of the views. **The Lookout** is perched on the edge of the estuary. It was designed by a Devon architect specialising in the use of green oak, Roderick James, and makes extensive use of timber. It sits well on its elevated site, which used to be occupied by a mussel purification plant. The wild life friendly garden was created by its owner.

Climbing further up the hill, we pass The Rag, or Jack the Lookout, a piece of ground on top of the (crumbling) cliff where fishermen used to watch for shoals of herring long ago. On the left we see another large recent house, **Salter House**, which replaces a modest brick built post-war bungalow. From the road, it is a somewhat forbidding composition of white rendered concrete, timber and glass, with a flat roof. It is strikingly different from the 1960s bungalows opposite. It was designed by Stan Bolt to make the most of the views over the estuary, Seen from the estuary, from it is a much more varied and friendly-looking house. It won the Daily Telegraph Contemporary House of the Year Award 2009.

Then we come to two large houses, one of modern build, behind great Victorian gateposts. The gateposts belonged to **Highcliffe**, which stands imposingly over lower Lympstone and looks out across the estuary on top of crumbling red cliffs. Among the owners, in Edwardian times, were Mrs. Cox and her two daughters, and it is due to them that the steep hill down to The Strand is called Cox's Hill by Lympstonians.. The Coxes were relations of Lord Roberts, the victorious General in the Boer War, and there is a photograph in the archives of Mrs. Cox in her ancient large-wheeled wheelchair, flanked by her daughters, with Lord Roberts visiting the Institute named in his honour, which the Coxes had paid for.

Until recently an old metal spiral stair led down from the clifftop garden at Highcliffe to the shingle below. One story has the butler escaping down this perilous stairway with the family silver. The late Ian Angus uncovered a granite cross in the churchyard with a panel inscribed: "In loving memory of Anne Wedderburn, daughter of the late Capt. James Cox, 92nd Gordon Highlanders… July 11th 1936", also of "her Sister, Jane Fanny Cox, died Oct. 1956, Aged 104 years and 9 months"! This beats the assumed village record of Captain Moilliet, later living to 100.

---

[1] Sowden House at one time owned an estate with much land round Sowden and in Longbrook Lane.

[2] A former owner saw a document stating that a Lady Mary de Pomfret owned the little manor in Henry III's lifetime (1216-1272), and in the Assize Rolls of 1330, one Herdewyn Bysouthedon paid taxes. As a sub-manor of Lympstone, Sowden would have had its local Lord. Like other small manor houses, it is partly built of pink random rubble sandstone.

[3] The beam is possibly a ship's mast, given that an old ship-breaking yard was once in the valley below Sowden Farm.

[4] Lords of the Manor and the clergy were said to be waiting customers, not averse to these duty-free goods and defrauding the Government of £2 million annually in Devon in the eighteenth century.

[5] *Trewman's Flying Post*, quoted in *Exmouth History*, by I. G. Cann & Robin Bush

[6] Barings Bank (1762-1995) was the oldest merchant bank in London until its collapse in 1995, after one of its employees, Nick Leeson, lost £827 million on speculative investing.

[7] He was also President of a mining company in Alberta, where the city of Lethbridge is named after him.

Chapter VI

From Cliffe Cottage to The Strand

Cliffe Cottage

This trim, rendered cottage dates from the early nineteenth century and has recognisably Regency windows with margin panes. It is roofed in slate and is probably built of brick under the render. There is a canopy over the fielded door.

A little further down the hill on the left is a house divided into nos. 1 and 2, with the name **Staffords** on them. The Staffords were important owners in the eighteenth century, and were relations of the Withalls. Like them, they sailed in the Newfoundland cod trade and brought salt fish back to Europe via the Azores. In the nineteenth century, they left for Exmouth and the family name dies out in the village earlier than the Withalls. There is also a **Stafford House** on the corner of Quay Lane, an imposing house with a hipped roof which was leased to Christopher Shears, mariner, in 1785, and left to innkeepers' wives and daughters in the nineteenth century. In the early years of the twentieth century it became an ironmonger's, and sold paraffin from its cellar. The shop window is a reminder of those days.

Looking down the Strand to Stafford House at the end

Quay Lane[1] then branches off to the left, an atmospheric part of old Lympstone paved with cobbles, and home to generations of fishermen and mariners even after the Great Fire of 1833. This burnt down 58 thatched cottages, making 240 people homeless (said to be the result of a fisherman cooking his mackerel at 5 am over a fire which set light to the chimney). They were eventually all rebuilt of brick.[2] Some have views across the estuary: **Sea View**, **Beach House** and **Highcliffe** have garden walls against which the high tide laps, as does **Watch House** with its anomalous 1960s flat roof extension. In the first three of these the old sail-making workshops can still be seen, now converted into kitchens.

Opposite the Lane on the east side, there is a row of early nineteenth century cottages, with six-pane Georgian windows. Then comes **The Globe Inn**, again early nineteenth century; which has held sway for generations, providing a cheerful fire, drink and food.[3]

Strand House

This detached house of about 1840 stands behind railings on the road. The symmetrical three-window range has sixteen panes in each, although the window above the central doorway is blocked: one window overlooks the water behind. Originally it was a double-depth plan, with principal rooms either side of the entrance door (with its rectangular fanlight), but the right-hand rooms have been knocked into one. Internally, it retains some of the fittings of the 1840s, including a dog-leg stair with stick balusters.

Built on to Strand House is a building with a striking pantiled hipped roof, perhaps a carriage house, with a single louvred window on the first storey and two double tall wooden doorways to the ground floor.

Then we notice **River Cottage**, facing away from the road and out to sea. It must have escaped the Great Fire of 1833. Inside, its great treasure is a sgraffito fireplace of extremely rare design. Most sgraffito patterns of the period were geometric, but this is a flower pattern, of which there are only four known examples remaining in England.

After this, we come to the **Lord Roberts Institute**, named after the victorious General of the Boer War,[4] who was also known for his Workshops, giving training and employment to ex-soldiers after the war. It is a tall red brick Edwardian building, with an oriel window onto the street and a timber framed gable. It was paid for by Mrs Cox of Highcliffe and her daughters, who were relations of the General.[5] Opened by the Bishop of Exeter (replacing Lord Roberts) in November 1907, it existed for the use of the parish "without distinction of class, politics or creed". After enlargement in 1913, it boasted a Hall and Assembly Room on its two floors, as well as a Reading Room, an Office and miniature Rifle Range, and hosted concerts, lectures, whist drives, billiards, tea parties and plays. Sold off in 1928, it was for a time The Strand Café, specialising in fish suppers, and more recently the Riverside Restaurant, before becoming two private dwellings.

Beyond the Institute lies what in the eighteenth century was the vast property of the Bass family, mariners, shipbuilders and resident in Lympstone since the fourteenth century.[6] They built quite large ships for the Navy in the Napoleonic wars, and their shipbuilding yard was on the Strand and the Green and the lane to Underhill. At one stage Worthington Brice, shipbuilder and entrepreneur, shared this yard, which reached back as far as the site on which the Methodist Chapel and schoolroom were later built. The bowsprit of one of his ships on the Green was so large it projected over the street by the bridge in to the opposite house.[7] There is still a building named Bass's there.[8]

After the Globe is a small cottage built of brick after the Great Fire, but with an ancient stone fireplace in the garden and the remains of old beams and screens inside. It is probably on the site of the old Poor House, overseen by Captain Williams of Sowden House, until legislation in the early nineteenth century resulted in the building of the St Thomas Union Workhouse at Exeter. There then appear on the east side more buildings, one of which was in use from the nineteenth century as a village bakery.[9]

Further down on the west side, Limekiln House, Slipway Cottage and the present Post Office form an area which is reputed to have been the old Manor Farm or Barton of the Suxpitches. This family farmed around the Clyst and Marsh Barton for around six hundred years, and also appeared in Lympstone. The name Suxpitch goes back to Saxon times, but unlike the Saxon Lord of Lympstone, the family stayed on through the Normans up to the early 19th century.

Limekiln House and Slipway Cottage

Limekiln House and Slipway Cottage were one dwelling until 1961. The building is largely early nineteenth century, although there is some fabric which dates probably from the seventeenth. It is a cob and stone mix, rendered, 12-pane sash windows. The cross wing is now a separate cottage, Slipway, which has a first floor two-light casement window, and an eighteenth century three-light attic window. Behind is a sensitively converted shed. On the shore are five limekilns, their outer wall forming part of the village's sea defences, punctuated by a pattern of circular holes. They are built of a mixture of sandstone, limestone and brick, and have

Limekilns

round-headed arches inside. Above them is the elevated garden of Limekiln House, with views across the estuary. A 1901 description of a freehold limekiln rented to George Clapp implies that one limekiln was working then. George Clapp died in the early 1900s, but he remembered the boats bringing limestone for burning in the kilns from the Babbacombe quarries, which they unloaded on the foreshore. At low tide, the stone was taken up to the kilns for burning by horse and cart. Tradition has it that the Sailing Club premises were then a stable.[10]

Limekiln House was, in the opinion of former residents, the Coventons, connected with smuggling, rife in Lympstone in the seventeenth, eighteenth and early nineteenth centuries.[11]

We next turn left down the narrow passage by the Post Office, the rear of which was part of the old stone Suxpitch House. Rising up on the left is Peter's Tower.

Peters Tower

Peters Tower dominates the foreshore, and is the defining landmark of the village, especially from the other side of the estuary where passing train travellers on their way to Cornwall can pick out Lympstone by its tower as they rush by.

It was built in 1885 by W. H. Peters, Esq of Harefield (*q.v.*), as the inscription tells us, "in Memory of his beloved wife Mary Jane, to commemorate her kindness and sympathy for the poor of Lympstone". Of red brick, with white brick used for its parapet and quoins, it is crenellated and machicolated in the manner of mediaeval Tuscan towers.[12]

Peters Tower

The windows are curved at the top, grouped in twos and threes, with a clock on two faces of the top storey. The four storeys are topped by a short lead spire with gabled belfry lucarnes to allow the clock chimes to be heard. It was most probably designed with the help of a pattern book by Mr Bass Sivell[13] of Lympstone, who supervised its building. The windows are curved at the top, grouped in twos and threes, with a clock on two faces of the top storey, the west facing one telling the fishermen when the tide was about to turn.

Inside, the tower contained a staircase and viewing platforms, and also a fireplace on the first floor to make it usable as a refuge for fishermen caught out in bad weather and unable to return to their homes.

By 1982 it was derelict, and the Peters family asked the Landmark Trust to take it over, to add it to their collection of interesting buildings that find a new use as holiday cottages. They replaced the rotten staircase with a replica of a Victorian spiral staircase, and based the interior accommodation on that of yachts, from galley kitchen to bunk beds.[14]

The external brickwork was in poor condition, but was fully restored and in some parts rebuilt. The clock chimes were silenced at night after complaints by the neighbours.

Together with the Tower, W. H. Peters built twelve cottages to be let to villagers at "a nominal rent", principally for "toilers of the deep". He demolished the fishermen's pub, The New Inn, with its skittle alley, to do so. The cottages form a terrace, also built of red brick, but now with their original fenestration altered and brickwork painted, although still with their wonderful view over the estuary. The area at the back of the cottages, with boatbuilding sheds and workshops, is one of the most atmospheric in Lympstone.

Returning to the Strand, past the Post Office (whose wrought-iron date of 1569 is not to be taken seriously) we go over what remains of the bridge over the Wotton Brook on its course to the river.

Bridge Cottages

Nos. 1-3 Bridge Cottages, have at their core an early eighteenth century house. On its side elevation, facing onto the Strand, is a shallow two-storey bow window. Built onto the front is a later shop building, with a hipped roof and a striking bowed shop window and door facing up the street.[15] **Nos. 4-5** run beside the Swan, and were built in 1840 onto the earlier cottages. Beyond is a former workshop and undertakers that later became a shopfitting business. Now converted into cottages, the whole row forms a most attractive little lane leading to the Sailing Club and Boat Shelter.

A nineteenth century shop window in Bridge Cottages

Beside the Sailing Club is a high, impressive stone wall with a curved bow. Here are more eighteenth century limekilns, with a 1920's bungalow, **Kilntop**, perched on top, with enviable views over the boat shelter and the estuary.

The Swan Inn

The Swan is an early nineteenth century building, with two canted bay windows with heavy moulded cornices to the ground floor, either side of the doorway. The porch has fluted pilasters, a cornice, and a rectangular fanlight. There is a lean-to extension to the right. After the coming of the railway in 1861, it was renamed the Railway Inn, but has since reverted to its original name. It was run in 1889 by George Chick, Mrs. Chick and their daughter, the late Tim Tapscott's mother. They made the pub's own beer in the long outbuildings behind, and also sold cider and wine.[16] Tim's grandfather, who had come from London, became the village undertaker, followed by his son. They had a workshop at the side of the Brook and behind the Swan. Tim later joined his father in this work, and knew where most of the village families had been buried in the churchyard, having a list of graves.[17] He also had a recipe for beer from his mother. In an old black

Field House

and white photograph of his, she can be seen standing by the wall of the Railway Inn, a handsome Victorian lady.

If you walk up the hill behind The Swan, towards Cliff Field, you pass a pair of brick semi-detached houses, built in 1911. Then on the right is another of Lympstone's recent architect-designed houses, **Field House**. The field on which it was built was let to the Devonshire Yeomanry before the First World War, and they built a Drill Hall and installed a Field Gun. The Drill Hall was only pulled down in the 1950s (it had long been used as the Village Dance Hall). The white modernist house that was erected in 2007 has a steel frame, rendered brick walls, and large areas of glass with wooden louvres. The living area is on the first floor, to take advantage of the views of the estuary. A striking composition, with clean lines and geometrically-placed windows, it is like a very large version of the Lescaze houses at Dartington, but topped by a fly-away roof. It was designed by the Suffolk architect Simon Conder, famous for his black rubber-clad house on the shingle at Dungeness. The partly-walled garden is a striking design by Patricia Stainton, using grasses and large seed heads in the manner of the Dutch pioneer of the New Perennial movement, Piet Oudolf.

1 Norman Mitchell, mariner, life-long Lympstonian and founder-member of the Sailing Club, said this lane was originally called Quarry Lane, owing to the quarried cliffs at its end.

2 Boat tackle, salt for curing fish, ropes and other goods were stored in the cellars or large sheds. It is said Ralph Lane, soldier and equerry to Elizabeth I lived at the end of Quay Lane, before going on Ralegh's expedition to the New World and founding an ill-fated colony on Roanoke Island in 1585. The colony was rescued by Sir Francis Drake on his return voyage.

3 An innkeeper of the Globe (Voysey) married Mary Ann, the sister of Richard Stafford. She became the landlady on his death in the 1870s. Her daughter Elizabeth Croft succeeded her.

4 Lord Roberts of Kandahar ("Bobs") commanded the British forces in Afghanistan in 1881-1882. He later became the Commander-in-Chief in India (1885-1893), in the South African War (1899-1902), and finally Commander-in-Chief of the British Army (1901-1904). He became known as 'Kipling's General', and Rudyard Kipling, a huge admirer, wrote two poems about him on his death.

5 There is a photograph of Lord Roberts with Mrs Cox in her Bath Chair and her three daughters, when he did visit Lympstone.

6 The Bass's acquired most of their property in Lympstone on the break-up of the manor in 1722. The wording of the Indenture has some interest: "… conveyed to John Bass, Shipwright, Dwellinghouses, Orchards and four acres of land also all the outhouses, courts courtilages Backsides Orchards Lands, Meadows … Ditches Waypaths Waters Watercourses etc. …Treasure Trove reserved."

7 This was before Worthington Brice went to Parsonage Stile House. Here he built and victualled whalers for Greenland, constructed tryworks for processing the whale oil, and built a landing stage for the ships and their cargo of blubber.

8 Further afield, the Basses owned Marsh Field (now the car park), Underhill, Hares, an applepound, a cottage called Bass's Orchard at Pretty Corner and a Bass's near the Swan pub. Their empire of four acres extended far in Lympstone.

9 The Bakery was run in the nineteenth century by the Sellers family, and in the twentieth notably by the Hodges.

10 Thos Suxpitch of Woodbury's will of 1832 refers to "houses and tenements… (in Lympstone) together with lime kilns and cellar lately bought of Mr. Bass". The Tithe Map of 1839 shows three cottages attached to Limekiln House, also shown

in a Francis Frith photograph of 1904. A Mortgage of 1901 describes "nine freehold cottages, two cellars, storeyard, workshop, old limekiln and garden".

[11] Tobacco and tubs were taken from Teignmouth over Lower Haldon to Powderham in the eighteenth century "where boats have been ready at any time after dusk ... to tow the Goods to Lympstone... a notorious haunt of Smugglers." Smuggling cost the Government £2 million per annum. Much of Devon's seamanship was exercised in the practice, which turned out first-class seamen.

[12] Imitating Italian towers was popular in the late nineteenth century, although this does not seem to be a copy of any one in particular.

[13] William Bass Sivell was described as "Architect" or "Gentleman".

[14] The lanterns in the living room and bathroom are copies of those on HMS Warrior, a nineteenth century battleship, which the Landmark Trust's founder, Sir John Smith, was helping to restore.

[15] This was at one time the National Provincial Bank. Across the road, the cottage now known as The Old Bank was Lloyds.

[16] This he lent to the late Ian Angus, who made a churchyard plan

[16] Alf Langmead remembered: "Us boys could always make a copper or two when they brewed up, because us used to have a two-wheel cart and could take the greens as they called it to people who had cattle in the village, which was quite a few, and not only that but people with gardens."

[17] This he lent to the late Ian Angus, who made a churchyard plan

Chapter VII

From the Swan to Burgmanns Hill

From The Swan Inn, the main village street passes the bottom of Station Hill, and then runs under the railway bridge. Just beyond, on the north side, are two major village houses, which would dominate the street - were they not half-hidden. The pathway that runs uphill between them was once the King's Highway, until the creation of Burgmanns Hill in the nineteenth century. The two houses may have been built as a pair, or one shortly after the other in imitation. Each has two rooms either side of the entrance hall, one room deep, with a service wing going off at right angles. It is their nineteenth century façades which disguise their similarity.

Queen Anne House

Behind an old brick wall and a thick laurel hedge lies Lympstone's first brick building.[1] It might indeed date from the reign of Queen Anne, for it is thought to have been built in 1702, the year she came to the throne (a datestone was found reset in the front garden wall). Red brick is the characteristic building material of the architectural style known as Queen Anne, a material that came to Devon comparatively late – the earliest brick building in the County is the Exeter Custom House of 1680/81.

The Queen Anne House is an imposing structure of Flemish bond under a slate roof. It has a grand entrance with a verandah, four Tuscan columns, pilasters, and two bow windows either side, which date from the early nineteenth century. There is one original window surviving in the right hand wall: the remainder are sashes put in c. 1840. Once there was a central gateway in the front garden wall, now blocked up. Two external brick chimney stacks support the gable ends.

The house was built by Thomas Smith, a wealthy merchant and mariner trading to Newfoundland. He and his grandson, Captain Thomas Smith, R. N., a naval hydrographer, were major figures in the Gulliford Meeting, the Dissenters' chapel. A collection of their letters has been found in the house, giving details of the Newfoundland trade in the eighteenth century and of naval hydrographic researches up to the 1830s – and some from India of a later date. They can be seen in the Devon Record Office.[2]

The Queen Anne House stands next to the railway line. In 1897, Mrs Julia Anne Walrond Davenport (*née* Smith) sold it to the Southern and Western Railway for use as the Stationmaster's House, "the grandest in all England".[3]

Queen Anne House

Bridgethorpe

Next door stands another grand half-hidden village house, Bridgethorpe, with an elegant stuccoed façade of two full-height canted bays, and a classical porch with square fluted Ionic columns. It too is built of brick and dates from the early eighteenth century – the façade is an 1840 addition.

This was a ship owner's house, belonging to the Withalls, who owned other land and property in Lympstone. The house was rented out at the end of the eighteenth century to Mary Gidoin, widow of the Vice-Admiral of the White, one of whose sons became Rector of Lympstone, and for a while she rented Varnes, another Withall house.[4]

The legend that Sir Digory Forest, who fought at Trafalgar, lived here is probably just that – for he is known to have lived at Ebford Mount, with its pineapple gateposts.[5] However the story of him driving his horses

Bridgethorpe

and carriage full pelt down the King's Highway beside Bridgethorpe into the village street, scattering villagers as he went, could well be true, as this was the main road to Exmouth, where he was building the first house on the Beacon.[6]

The memories of Fanny Orchard, who lived at Bridgethorpe as a child at the end of the nineteenth century, speak of a lovely house, a Gentleman's house, in grounds. Front and back stairs led to kitchen quarters, divided from the living rooms by green baize doors. There was a courtyard with several outhouses. Stone steps led to the stables and coach house and footman's quarters, and to a large railed-in and walled fruit garden and a greenhouse. Up the stone steps was a vegetable garden, with a croquet lawn behind. Beyond that came a tennis court and then waste land. The courtyard and outhouses are still there, but the coach house has become a separate house, and the grounds have been sold off. Fanny remembers climbing onto the front wall at Bridgethorpe to watch the torchlight processions for the Relief of Ladysmith and of Mafeking during the Boer War. She was also there when Queen Victoria died.[7]

The grand-daughter of the next owner, the Revd Dr Fortescue Webb, married the author Eden Phillpotts, whose novel *Redcliffe* is based on Lympstone.[8] Another romantic story is that of a secret smugglers' passage leading to the river.[9]

Opposite Bridgethorpe's drive, there is an alley-way leading to Marsh Path Cottage and the Brook. Some of the houses along this stretch behind the Strand are very interesting, in that they have formed a square courtyard behind it, and have attics or box rooms which inter-connect. Lamb's Cottage and Melody Cottage have them, together with Deeds showing that Lamb's Cottage is near or on the site of "a Chapel or Meeting House for Divine Worship", which was there in 1761.[10]

Honeysuckle Cottage & Morton

"Down the village street there is a small house built of red bricks mellowed by time and weather. It stands almost on the road itself, its bow window jutting out over the cobbled kerb," wrote a Lympstone diarist, Annie Thomas, at the end of the nineteenth century.[11] She was describing Honeysuckle Cottage, which was a china shop then, and in the early years of the twentieth century a dairy. Morton Cottage next door, with its projecting window elegantly curved at the corners, was a hardware shop, which did a roaring trade in paraffin. Honeysuckle is a double depth plan and extends towards the courtyard at the back. It has an unusual feature, a staircase rising in two stages, or a double stair. Most of the attic space is a

Honeysuckle Cottage and Morton, with their shop bay windows

flying freehold over Morton. All the walls are completely straight, as is the very big chimney stack to the rear, which is shared with Morton. The brickwork is in fine condition, in Flemish bond.

The china shop at Honeysuckle was kept by Mrs Clara Parsons, according to Annie Thomas's charming memoir. Clara was a widow who had come to Devon from her Dorset home. She was a first cousin of Thomas Hardy and "in her features the strong lines of the Family Face were clearly marked. Her son Harry was scarcely five feet tall, but he had a fine head crowned with dark, curly hair and through his temperament, his perseverance and the obvious sparks of genius within him he could certainly have been said to bear some resemblance to his famous relative."

Harry was a postman, who owned a bicycle on which he made his rounds of outlying farms and villages, delivering post and newspapers, which in the days before radio and television were eagerly awaited. "When Thomas Hardy's *Tess of the D'Urbervilles* was serialised in the Graphic, people would hurry out to their doors and ask, 'They'll never hang that girl, will they Harry?'"

Harry was also a musician, the church organist and a member of the village band. He gave music lessons and his trio supplied the music for weekly dances in the town and for those village halls around. "Harry is now but a memory of the village life of a bygone age, but when the older generations talk of past events and pleasures he must inevitably come to mind: the Saturday Night Penny Concerts, when he organised and accompanied the varied programme every week: the Maypole dances and the Morris dance music for the Harvest Festival, the choral performances in the church and the Drill Hall concerts of World War One when he persuaded all manner of celebrities to come and take part. 'Harry will be there,' people would say. 'It's going to be grand: we can leave it all to Harry'".[12]

Osborne House & Ferndale

This pair of nineteenth century brick houses share a surprising façade – surprising because the windows have Gibbs surrounds[13], an unusual feature for a village street. On closer inspection, it turns out that they are not of projecting stone, but white paint on the brickwork, a decorative addition. When was this done? It certainly makes for a lively façade. A feature of the brickwork is tuck pointing - the mortar is mixed with brick dust to make it the same colour as the bricks, and a thin line of white plaster inserted to give the appearance of particularly fine mortar work, a technique more often found in Bloomsbury than in a Devon village.[14]

Osborne House and Ferndale with their attractive pair of fanlights

Side by side are two most attractive door lights, an oblong one with a diagonal cross on Osborne, and a pretty traceried fanlight on Ferndale, which also has a peg slate roof. Osborne has a projecting shop window, and the sign high on its gable end reads 'W. H. Reynolds, Carriage Proprietor', although an old photograph shows that it was originally J. Osborne who ran the business. Inside the yard, reached by a double gate, was the old workshop where the carriages were made, now converted to a two-storey detached cottage. The outlook over the wall is a great backdrop of trees, both ornamental, such as copper beech and willow, and everyday conifer. It is a great surprise after the busy street front. There is a revealing Edwardian photograph of this part of Lympstone, with boys with caps and scuffed shoes, and with a horse and cart coming down the unmetalled road. Glad Hawkins kept a shop here, full of little bits of everything.

Across the road is an interesting complex of cottages, some of them listed, and what was once a lane, parallel to the lane beside Bridgethorpe, going up towards the Avenue and the road on to Exton and Exeter. These were the main ways of getting up to the higher ground before Colonel Burgmann built Lady Burgmann's Hill, which forks left at the end of the Strand. This second lane is now private.

Jasmine Cottage

Set back from the Strand and behind railings, Jasmine Cottage used to be part of Burn's Tenement in the early nineteenth century when it was built, although it may incorporate earlier work. Built of random rubble sandstone and limestone, with a slate roof, it is of single-depth plan, with added rooms to the back, from which the small garden area can be seen. To the right of the front door is a sixteen-pane sash window. This is a beautiful old cottage with its exposed stonework and prominent window, surrounded by a small front garden with flowering shrubs and climbers. It may once have been a bakehouse.

Up the lane there is an area once used as the drying ground for the cottages, now belonging to Midships, with some sheds. In the nineteenth and twentieth centuries these sheds were used as workshops, and later still as the football changing rooms

To the left of Jasmine Cottage is a three-storey brick house, now known as Clays, which a sailmaker owned in the nineteenth century. It is thought he lived at Jessamine as there was an old connecting door, now blocked off. The sail-loft ran the length of the house.

Clay's Cottage

This mid-nineteenth century cottage, built of random rubble limestone, has a picturesque appearance, with rambling roses and climbers round the twentieth century porch. A wall of 'pobbles' divides it from Jasmine on the other side of the path. Widely found in Budleigh, pobbles are rare in Lympstone. It has a red pantiled roof, and is of two storeys.

A splendid feature is the external projection on the higher end of the house, which was originally a stair turret, it is thought, leading to the first floor at the rear of the hall of a fifteenth/sixteenth century house. This house would have been a three-room cross-passage one, of which the passage and service room have been destroyed, but are survived by the hall and inner room, now separate cottages. The staircase would have been inserted with the first floor in the late sixteenth century. There are horizontally sliding windows, some with wooden sill pegs.

1, Clays Cottages and Farleys[15]

All the Clays Cottages look old, picturesque and intriguing up this small private lane, which now has no apparent end or reason. Their stonework shows something of their age, and is mellow, uneven and attractive. They are built of cob on random rubble footings, and have been dated to the 1400s, or early 1500s. These two were a part of a former cross-passage house with three rooms, being the hall and inner room respectively. The original roof of the inner room has been demolished, as has the cross-passage and service end. The medieval roof of the hall, however, survives, with a nineteenth century roof over it. The old roof would have been thatched. Smoke-blackened beams show that there was a central hearth below, from which the smoke rose unimpeded. The hall appears to have been constructed of one bay only. While the two-storeyed inner room was partitioned off from the hall, the truss was not closed, and so smoke filtered through and lightly blackened the inner room. In later years, a smoke bay of cob and wattle was put in near the left side truss. The medieval roof has a diagonal ridge piece, two trusses, possibly jointed crucks, with the purlins and rafters all smoke-blackened. The first floor would have inserted in the late sixteenth century, reached by the stair turret that became part of Clay's Cottage, under a catslide.

Fern Cottage & Hope Cottage

This divided farmhouse of the late sixteenth century has become two cottages, sitting back from the curving end of the Strand where it forks to become Burgmanns Hill. The cottages have pretty wisteria and flowering

cherries in their small front gardens, and present a uniform appearance, being built of roughcast cob, block-plastered to the front.

Originally, the building was of single depth, and there are the remains of an exterior chimney stack at the rear. The two cottages were remodelled in the nineteenth century. There are the remains of an exterior chimney stack at the back of Fern Cottage, and also of a small courtyard under the present kitchen. Of great interest is the thatch found in the space between the old roof and the nineteenth one.[16] A large jointed cruck runs the length of the two cottages. In Hope Cottage there is an eighteenth century rear wing to the service end, timber framed with brick noggin, and nineteenth century casement windows. The roof space is ceiled, but the lower members of the hall crucks are visible.

One of the first known owners of the house was a chemist and druggist. It kept its medical connection when a distinguished Exeter surgeon and philanthropist bought the orchard, John Haddy James, who had been at Trafalgar with Nelson, and later founded a hospital in Paris.

Thornbury & Little Thornbury
Up a short drive, the façade mostly hidden from the road, lies a low elegant house, now separate dwellings, built in the late sixteenth century.

Thornbury

Thornbury had been a three-room, through passage type of house, with a rear range added later. The second end chimney stack to the right is now swallowed up in a much later house at the beginning of Burgmanns Hill.

It is of random rubble to the front and cob to the rear. It has been altered considerably during the nineteenth century, including its frontage, which is distinguished by its cluster of windows - two deeply canted bays either side of the left hand entrance, and 20-paned tripartite sashes on the two storeys, making a lively composition. There are six jointed crucks in the roof with a diagonal ridge-piece, which date from the house's origins in the late sixteenth century. Built as a farmhouse, on the slopes above the much wider and deeper Brook, it encroached on to the Waste, or the Lord of the Manor's rabbit warrens, called in 1796 'the Burrows'.

Thornbury was still one house when a London Dutch merchant, George Burgmann, came to Lympstone and bought it in 1822. He and his family enjoyed the house, which at that time was on the corner of the Strand and the small Vicarage Road, a narrow lane, with no room for two carriages to pass. The main Exmouth-Exeter road at the time ran from the Marsh on up past Bridgethorpe, with hardly room for a packhorse. Sir George (as he became) gave some land to enable a new road to be built, which he named Lady Burgmann's Hill.[17]

[1] There was a block of tenements on this site in the 17th century. This house was originally called The Brick House. Bricks as building material first arrived at ports – Topsham (for Exeter) and Lympstone.

[2] Thomas Smith's father and family had long farmed Thorn Farm on the now A376.

[3] Before the Railway, the Queen Anne House had been owned by Mrs. Julia Anne Walrond Davenport Smith. She also owned all the land from her house up to the end of the Strand, and behind these houses up to the Avenue of trees on Burgmann's Hill. She was related to the Walronds of Bovey and thought little of the Rolles of the time, giving it as her opinion they were descended from "ostlers in Wales"!

[4] Her second son, John Lewis Gidoin was also in holy orders, and worked in the Parish with the Rector, John Prestwood Gidoin.

[5] Pineapples became popular as finials, particularly on gateposts, after the first English pineapple was grown at Hampton Court in the reign of Charles II.

[6] The earliest Deed known is of 1763, of Richard Withall making provision for his wife and children. In 1772 there was a sale to the Revd. Thomas Clarke of Woodbury for "All that Messuage and Tenement, a large Brick Dwellinghouse with its Appertuances wherein dwelt John Withall at time of his death, And of a lot of Old Earth and separated by the King's Highway from the house in which Thomas Smith lately dwelt, and also the Plott of Ground towards the Garden Wall of that Dwellinhouse which extends from the necessay house to the King's Highway…"

[7] Fanny Orchard also remembers visiting Nutwell Court, her mother being a friend of Miss Hudson, the housekeeper, when the owners were away. They were given a cream tea and later shown round the great rooms, where she saw a piece of Sir Francis Drake's ship The Golden Hind, and a bed on which Sir Walter Raleigh had slept.

[8] Ralph Rochester has researched Eden Phillpotts, giving a talk 'Redcliffe Revisited' in the village hall, in which he said that though they met in Lympstone, Robina and the author never lived in the village. After his death, she returned to Candys.

[9] Another discovery in the house has been that of an 'underground passage' leading from the cellar below a hall cupboard, which was full of noxious fumes when explored.

[10] This discovery in an Indenture has added to Lympstone's history, as previously the only known village dissenters' chapel was the Unitarian Chapel by Ellenthorpe, now destroyed.

[11] Annie Margaret Thomas, née White, lived in the Belvedere when a child. Her parents came to live there on the invitation of Nutwell Court's owners in the early twentieth century.

[12] Harry Parsons was self-taught, which makes his activities all the more remarkable.

[13] A Gibbs surround was named after the great eighteenth century architect James Gibbs, who often employed the effect of a stone banded architrave round windows and doors, though usually with a massive keystone at the top, which this painted version does not have.

[14] But see also Sheppards. The Bloomsbury squares were designed by C. P. Cockerell, the architect of Nutwell Court.

[15] These houses were divided from one in 1974. (originally 2 and 3 Clays Cottages). Miss Farley lived in both parts as one.

[16] One of six such roofs found in Lympstone.

[17] After the Burgmanns, Thornbury was sold to a man whose daughter was marrying a young officer in the Royal Devon Garrison Artillery. The cautious father entailed the house to any children of the marriage. That young officer, however, appears (in a Directory) as Major-General Dick and family, so there had been no cause for anxiety! The General's daughter, Miss Augusta Dick, became not only the Hon. Secretary of the Tennis Club but also of the Lending Library.

Chapter VIII

From Burgmanns Hill to Nutwell Lane

The higher slopes of Lympstone towards the old Rectory were a magnet for the wealthy health-seekers and house-builders of the eighteenth century. Once Lady Burgmanns Hill was created, the carriage trade could pass with ease and move up and down the hill from the old Rectory (now Hayes Raleigh), which had been there since the sixteenth century.

Lining the initial slope of Burgmanns Hill are many newer buildings. Greenhill Avenue, which breaks off to the right, was known as 'the Undopted' before War, when the white concrete house, **Michaelhouse**, stood alone in the middle, with Captain Moilliet looking out from its tower with his telescope. The Avenue was completed after the war, when the meadowland was no longer required for growing swedes.

After this, the road levels out, and we reach the first of the big houses built at the end of the eighteenth century.

Greenhill and Higher Greenhill

This handsome pair of brick houses has been built to suggest a single large dwelling, with an entrance doorway in the middle, framed by a porch with a barrel vault. In fact there is a second entrance for Higher Greenhill discreetly to one side. The windows of the *piano nobile* are round-headed, the brickwork is of Flemish bond, and all is topped by a Romantic castellated parapet, which hides two slate hipped roofs. The whole composition could be described as sternly picturesque. The back elevation is a surprise, slate-clad with two round-headed Gothick windows, but it is not easily seen from any public space.

Inside there are panelled doors and internal shutters. Both houses have staircases on their left-hand sides, rising to the third floor, and which are of fine workmanship, made of oak, with a rail of inlaid walnut.

The garden with its mature trees is enclosed in a high brick wall, but two houses have recently been built within it.

Like the Manor House, the Greenhills were built to let out to wealthy visitors seeking the balmy climate of the South West to restore their health. In the last years of the eighteenth century and the early years of the nineteenth, they were prevented by the Napoleonic Wars from travelling abroad.

The house next door, however, is much older in origin.

Greenhill and Higher Greenhill

Merrylands

The plain dignified front, with its large nineteenth century sash windows and parapet, does not speak of the farmhouse that this once was. But the garden front tells a different story. Here you see cob and leaded windows, the oldest with ninety six lights, in an attractive asymmetrical façade dating from the late eighteenth/early eighteenth century. This was the farm of the Glebe, belonging to the Rectorial Manor. The seventeenth century part was of a single depth, with a rear wing, and the main rooms on either side of the central hall. The external end stacks have shafts of the usual small imported seventeenth century Dutch bricks, as elsewhere in the village.

Inside there are still some seventeenth century fittings, notably three panelled doors, a built-in dresser with a moulded cornice, a fireplace with a herringbone pattern brick back, a pine overmantel in the kitchen, and a 17th century staircase, formerly enclosed in an external stair turret.

There have been some notable inhabitants. It was one of the houses in which, before the Act of Toleration in 1690, Unitarian or Presbyterian meetings were held. In 1760 it was occupied by John Filmore, Master Mariner, and became known as Filmore's. He was succeeded by

The older garden front of Merrylands, with the Gothick window of Greenhill to the left

Lady Lewin, whose soldier son was sent to guard Napoleon when he was first captured and sent to Elba. The story goes that he changed places with another Lympstone officer, but that Napoleon spotted it. In the early 19th century, now called Avenue House after the avenue of lime trees opposite which still line the path to Cliff Field, it became the home of Wakelin Welch, who was a benefactor of Lympstone schools and the church. His business interests in America included being an agent for George Washington, buying English goods and selling them over there. His wife, Elizabeth Welch, endowed a little school, and she erected a plaque in her husband's honour in the village school.[1] Wakelin Welch had a famous legal argument with the Drakes of Nutwell over the allocation of pews in the parish church. He won the argument but lost the pews.

An eminent physician, Dr Seward, changed the name of the house to Merrylands in the middle of the last century. He spent much time creating a garden,[2] in which he held parties, Flower Shows and Conservative Fetes, but he sold off part of it for the building of Well House. The garden is once again one of the glories of Merrylands.

The pine overmantel in the kitchen at Merrylands

The Manor House

There is a 1920s drawing of The Manor House by Miss Lilian Sheldon[3] which shows vividly this formal Georgian house with its symmetry and external shutters, surrounded by trees and shrubs. Little has changed from the outside, although a catastrophic fire in 1990 destroyed the roof and caused much internal damage. The building is now restored as flats.

The façade takes it character from its red bricks in Flemish bond, and from the pattern of louvred East Devon sliding shutters, with their frilly top battens. It was built in 1760, an imposing three-storey house with a parapet. It has a symmetrical front, with bay windows on either side of the central projecting bay. On the ground floor there are two rectangular bays with parapets and a central entrance over which the ironwork parapets are carried. To either side of the bay windows there are open ironwork verandahs, probably of the nineteenth century, one of which is glazed.

The Manor House

Built to be let, The Manor House was leased in 1809 to one of the invalids who used to come to Lympstone for its health-giving air during the Napoleonic wars. She was Lady Williamina Forbes from Edinburgh, whose tale is so poignantly told by Ralph Rochester in his book *For Love of Williamina*. She was loved by two remarkable men: James Mill the philosopher and father of John Stuart Mill; and the great poet and novelist Sir Walter Scott, who wooed her for seven years before she rejected him. She appears in many guises in Scott's writing, and he never forgot her. She married instead the wealthy Sir William Forbes of Pitsligo, but after giving birth to five children she contracted tuberculosis, in those days incurable. On medical advice her husband brought her all the way to Devon by coach. The "modern dwelling house" that they rented "had a coach house, stables, cellars and a walled garden with adjoining orchard". Williamina found her "little residence" in Lympstone "very charming", and the rooms small but comfortable. Sadly, after two years, she died here, surrounded by her husband and parents.

In 1922 The Manor House was sold out of the Rectory Glebe to Gilbert Sheldon, a poet and novelist, and his sister Lilian, who looked after him, for he was an invalid, having suffered from polio as a child. He was famous for his book *From Trackway to Turnpike*, which became the standard work on English roads. Lilian, who was eight years older, took a first in Natural Sciences at Newnham College, Cambridge, and later trained as an artist. Although there were only two of them in such a large house (with servants), the Sheldons lived in style, dressing formally for dinner every evening. Lympstone has particular reason to be grateful to them, as they gave Avenue Field and Cliff Field to the National Trust for public use.[4] With some searching, Gilbert Sheldon's grave can be found in the churchyard.

Hayes Raleigh

Brick gate piers frame the entrance to the driveway, and a shrubbery greets you, so that the house is at first hidden, surrounded by numerous graceful trees. The house itself is a remodelling in 1700 of an older one, and there is still evidence of this to be found inside. If you go down the drive, you find the entrance front facing south, but the main room with its big square bay looks out across the estuary to the Haldon Hills.

Hayes Raleigh is mostly built of brick, but plaster rendered, the crosswing in sandstone, a left-hand extension in plastered cob. An east wing was added in the nineteenth century, when most of the house was refenestrated with sash windows, although some leaded casements from 1700 survive to the rear.

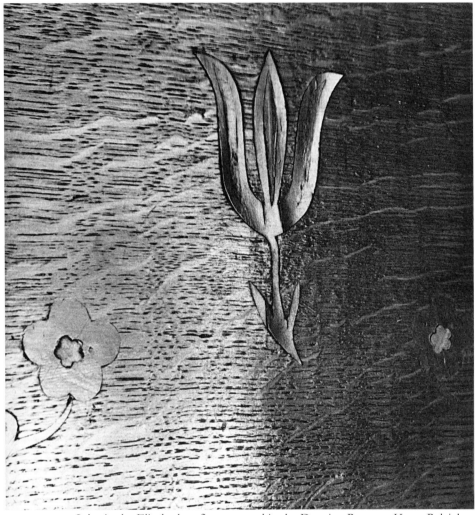

Inlay in the Elizabethan fire surround in the Drawing Room at Hayes Raleigh

There is much of interest inside: panelling in the cross passage and the principal room, which has a plaster ceiling with a simple attractive roundel. The old wooden fire surround and overmantel in this room retains the original cornice and Ionic capitals, with some delicate inlay. A nineteenth century fireplace in the dining room has kept some beautiful Delft tiles, with river and canal scenes, sailing boats and barges. The oak dog-legged staircase has a panelled dado and a cornice. An old well survives in the back passage, now lit and glazed, as do some old windows with thick glazing bars, and a cruck truss upstairs from the pre-1700 house.

Plaster roundel in the ceiling at Hayes Raleigh

From at least 1616, when it was "in the possession of Isiayah Farrington Parson of the said Parish" (in the words of the Glebe Terrier), this was the Parsonage and then Rectory. In the eighteenth century, a roaming parson, the Revd. John Swete, rode over many ways and byeways in Devon, painting as he went (he managed eighteen Volumes). He came through Lympstone in 1799, and stopped to paint a beautiful picture of The Parsonage and also of the Darling Rock in Romantic fashion, against the backdrop of the fishermen's cellars and the foreshore (no boat shelter yet). His work gives us a real flavour of what the small leafy village was then like, and something of life at that time, though with romantic exaggeration.

Just beyond Hayes Raleigh, where the road bends before the gates to Belvedere, we find a rough lane to Parsonage Stile. Down by the river until 1832 (when it was destroyed by fire) was Parsonage Stile House, said to have been an inn, the haunt of smugglers. It then became the home of the shipowner, Worthington Brice, when he bought it from the (impoverished) Drake owner. Here he built a landing stage and tryworks on becoming the driving force behind the whaling project in the eighteenth century.

Nutwell Court and Belvedere

Strictly speaking, neither Belvedere nor Nutwell Court are within the Lympstone boundary, which goes down to Parsonage Stile. But it seems legitimate to say a little about them, as Woodbury and Lympstone Parish were at one time part of Nutwell Manor, which had absorbed them both. Furthermore, these houses are geographically part of Lympstone, not Woodbury, and have interacted so much with our village, that it would be pedantic to omit them.

Nutwell Court was founded in the twelfth century, when Henry I gave Geoffroy de Dinan two manors in Devon, Harpford and Nutwell. These became the property of Olivier de Dinan, who built "a fine castle and chapel". In the fifteenth century Lord Dinham of Nutwell became Treasurer and advisor to the Kings of England. He lived in office through the reigns of three kings without being beheaded, a mighty feat of diplomacy in those days.

The house we glimpse today from the cycle path, surrounded by a wonderful collection of mature trees and with a large pond in front, was rebuilt in 1802 to a design by the architect Samuel Pepys Cockerell, whose best known works were the Bloomsbury Squares in London and Sezincote House in Gloucestershire. Pevsner describes Nutwell as "an exquisitely precise and austere classical mansion", although he says that the loss of the glazing bars from the windows make it seem excessively dour.[5] It is a remodelling of a much older house, with a nineteenth century chapel on the site of the chapel licensed here in 1371.

We can visit Nutwell at the end of the nineteenth century in the company of Annie Thomas, who lived as a child at The Belvedere, which her parents rented. "Lady Drake was the ruler of the little kingdom set like a fortress within its high brick walls, the entrance drives hidden by massive wooden doors which were jealously guarded by the lodge-keepers at either end of the estate, like priests at the approach to some sacred shrine. 'What is it you want?' they would enquire of the hawker or stranger opening the doors. 'Oh, no! The Ladyship wouldn't allow me to let you inside,' for she was always The Ladyship, and her orders were simply given and firmly enforced.

"Sometimes she would call to inspect the trees in the avenue, for trees were her great delight and the woods and park of Nutwell still bear witness to her care and planning, as they rise rich and green from the banks of the Exe estuary.

Belvedere

"Sometimes in her absence my sister and I would be allowed to visit Nutwell where the housekeeper would give us tea, with butter and cream from Home Farm and luscious helpings of quince jam, and afterwards we would peep at the lovely rooms beyond. Amid a wealth of art treasures the drawing-room was dominated by Van Dyke's portrait of the great Elizabethan Sir Francis... One of the guest rooms was the Armada Room, papered in soft sea green with imposing fleets of galleons around the frieze and a four-poster bed of quite incredible size!"[6]

A later owner of Nutwell was George Vernon Northcott, who made a fortune out of DIY, and who, through his charitable trust, provided the money to build the Northcott Theatre in Exeter, named after him.

Belvedere was built as an eighteenth century folly tower, facing Haldon Belvedere on the other side of the estuary. It is battlemented, with a large protruding bay. It was added onto the older farmhouse of Nutwell, some of which survives at the back. Annie Thomas as a child saw in an old attic room under the roof the deeply cut letters "A. S. 1747" and another date from the 1600s. She describes going from the main house to the much earlier back, through the servants' quarters and kitchen. When Lady Drake visited, "little girls were neither to be seen or heard".[7]

The large two storey wing was added to the house by Mrs Clarke, when she moved from Nutwell Court in the 1960s. It is also battlemented and has big sliding windows.

The Lodge at the entrance to Belvedere is remarkable for its castellated and turreted chimney, with a large key. Together they symbolize the victory at Gibraltar by the father of the second Lord Heathfield, who had it built.

---

[1] He is also remembered in the church porch for a charity he set up for delivering blankets to the poor of the village.

[2] Dr. Seward did much of the gardening himself, helped by his gardener, Charlie Stephens, who lived at Metherells.

[3] In 2003, a painting by Lilian hung in the Sailing Club, one of many from this good, but not outstanding artist.

[4] This is from a paper also given by Ralph Rochester, who obtained much of his information about the Sheldons from the late Bishop of Exeter, Dick Cartwright, who knew them well.

[5] Sir Nikolaus Pevsner, author of the great series of guides to *The Buildings of England*. The Devon volume was revised by Bridget Cherry in 1986, and is still available.

[6] "Upstairs too were some of the very early family portraits which we found rather frightening – it was reputed that one of them was haunted, and several people had seen the eyes move! Be that as it may, the Rector of Lympstone was called in to deal with the matter and everyone was satisfied."

[7] Annie Thomas concludes, "As the old order changed and yielded place to the new, Lady Drake quietly passed from a world which she could never have comprehended, The Ladyship to the end."

Chapter IX

From Chapel Lane to Underhill and the Mill

We now return to the side roads which wind off the main artery of the village. Chapel Road used to be a private track, with a gate shutting it off after a few houses near the top. It was called The Private up until the Second World War. **The Primitive Methodist Chapel**[1] was built down here in 1883 (on piles, as the ground was so boggy from the then much wider and deeper Wotton Brook). It is built of limestone in a crazy paving design, with tall cusped lancet windows clustered around the porch and along both sides, and a trefoil window in the gable. The Foundation Stone tells us that the builder was Mr R. Venman and the architect C. L. Abbott, *Esq.*[2] Next to it stands the smaller red brick **Primitive Methodist Schoolroom**, with white bricks decorating the arches of its round-headed windows and quoins. Heavy bargeboarding decorates the gable and the porch. A stone name strap on the façade tells us the building's function, the letters cut in an austere *sans serif* face.[3] In the eighteenth century this was the site of some of the Bass's shipbuilding berths by the Brook, which Worthington Brice, ship builder and whaler, for some time shared. Next to the chapel and schoolhouse is a brick Victorian terrace.

The first house that faces us at the end of the road is Underhill House, called Underhill Tenement in the late eighteenth and early nineteenth centuries, meaning 'property' or 'dwelling someone owned'.[4]

Underhill House and Kilrush

The two bows of Underhill House rise gracefully to three storeys, white-washed with black painted features. It dates from about 1810. The central doorway has pilasters and a half-glazed door with a semi-circular fanlight. There are hornless sash pane windows to the first and second floors in this central bay. All in all, it is a later Georgian house of some gravity and elegance, its symmetry only slightly spoiled by the little extension to the right hand front, built in the 1990s when the house was divided.

Beautifully hand-painted nineteenth century flower and bird panels decorate some interior doorways, which were once taken down but fortunately found by a passer-by and rescued for the present owner.

Later in the nineteenth century, Kilrush, a three-storey one-bay house with tripartite windows, was inserted between Underhill House and Metherells, and as a consequence, one of Underhill's chimneystacks is now shared with Kilrush. It makes for an impressive sequence of tall chimneys.

The two-storey bow window of Underhill House

It appears that Underhill House was part of the vast Bass empire in Lympstone, and that John Bass lived there.[5] In 1873 the owner of Underhill, William Bass Sivell,[6] bought a strip of land in front of his house to plant a quickset hedge, "so far as possible to shut out from view the cottages opposite to the dwellinghouse". This land later became vegetable gardens, but is now the site of bungalows and two recently-built houses.

A detail of a painted door in Underhill house

Metherells[7]

Metherells presents a handsome symmetrical façade of two bays, either side of a grand porch with a deep cornice supported by Tuscan columns. The door is semi-glazed, with a wide arching fanlight. Four tripartite sash windows, and a smaller window above the porch. The hipped roof is of slate, with a raked two-light dormer. On the left is a large exterior stack with a tall chimney. That on the right is subsumed in Kilrush, which has squeezed in beside it. The house dates from the early years of the eighteenth century, but the details of the façade must be nineteenth century.[8] Built onto the back is a tall one-room deep brick extension. In the middle of the entrance hall stands a beautiful staircase of about 1800, with

Metherells, the portico

a continuous curved open stair with wreathed rails rising the full height of the house.

There are some panelled doors of the early eighteenth century, and nineteenth century panelled shutters. We know from early indentures that Captain Henry Metheral built the house when all the surrounding land was meadow, with the much wider, deeper Brook running across it towards the River by the Strand.[9]

Originally, the house was thatched, and possibly of the two-room, through-passage type. The Dairy mentioned in the deeds was a small outbuilding to the left of Metherells' drive, partially of cob, and recently refurbished.

Notable owners of the house such as Thomas Hussey of Highcliffe, followed by his sister, Viscountess Chetwynd, were later replaced by less aristocratic villagers: Frederick George Venus, fishmonger, Thomas Bowerman who had the Dairy, Charles Frederick Venus, shopkeeper, Walter John Norton, a railway signalman, Charles Malcolm Stephens, gardener, and Kathleen Mary Stephens who ran a small home for invalids in Metherells, and took in laundry.

Now we continue down Underhill, passing under a railway bridge built of brick laid in English bond, passing a 1970s housing estate on our right and the Brook on our left, where in spring every year appears a notice: "SLOW DOWN! FROGS CROSSING!" There on the right, above its splendid gardens on the hillside, stands the old Underhill Farmhouse, now hemmed in on both sides and behind by estate houses where once there were trees and agricultural fields.

The Sanctuary and Sunnybank

Underhill Farmhouse (now divided into two dwellings) is a cob and thatch house of the sixteenth century. It is still thatched, with a large stack and tall chimney in the middle of its façade, and lies half-way up the steep hillside, with beautiful gardens in front, layered with colourful flowers and shrubs. It was once presumably consciously well out of the tides of the Wotton Brook, which now flows quietly by below. People living in the lower houses on the estate find pebbles in their soil, washed in by the then much higher water. Once there were many shipbuilding yards along this brook as far as the Mill, and boats were floated down it to reach the Exe on a high tide.

Originally the farmhouse was a three-room through-passage house with the kitchen or service end to the right, and a parlour in the rear wing.

The Sanctuary and Sunnybank, formerly Underhill farmhouse

The hall was heated by its prominent front stack, which has brick shafts. The rear inner room was not heated. In the late nineteenth century a brick extension was added, as were some windows. Beneath the present internal partitions, there may be surviving screens; there are upper crucks to the main range. An upstairs internal beam could even date from the fifteenth century. A large inglenook fireplace has been discovered underneath three others.

This thatched dwelling is one of the tucked-away treasures of the village, standing for centuries in its own land.

We continue on down the lane to its junction with Church Path, a small lane lined with houses on one side, leading up to the right over the hill to the Sowden area. To the left is the drive to **Orchard Dene**, a hidden detached house, and beside it Sheppards Lane, which runs up to the main village road. But we go straight on along a winding, wooded path till we come to the Mill Field through a kissing gate.

The Mill

Across the field, sheltered by tall ancient trees, stands Lympstone Mill, in the midst of tranquil meadows, at the bottom of a hill. This is Lympstone at its most rural. There is an old photograph showing a long, low thatched cob building of uncertain date. The same building still stands, though there have been changes since that earlier photograph, including the demolition (following a fire) of a barn to the left. Slate has replaced thatch, and we now see two gable ends with barge boarding. The smaller has been extended forward some fifteen feet in brickwork. A front porch has been added. All is plastered and pinkwashed.

The Mill building itself is to the right, and was extended after the old photograph was taken. When the original mill stream began to dry up, a leat was built bringing water from the Brook into a mill pond which still exists. The first rooms were used for drying the malt and contained ovens to process it. Then comes the Mill machinery, and outside, at the end, an overshot water wheel. In the field next to the Mill is the quarry[10] that provided the stone for the church re-building in 1409.

The Mill, Christmas 2010

The nineteenth century mill machinery

The first documented record of a mill here is in 1254, when "William's Mill" was mentioned in a dispute in the Royal Court at Westminster. The next possible record of a miller is in 1399, when John Hoppyng was under threat of excommunication "because he has brewed once and broken the assize of beer - in mercy 4d."[11] In 1525 we have evidence of the Mill in a Survey of all the Lands of Cecily, Marchioness of Dorset, Lady Harington and Bonville.[12] In this Survey of her Lympstone inheritance, we find that the tenants of "one water grist mill with one meadow" were Phillip, James and Thomas Fulford, and John Wright, at an annual fixed rent of 26s.8d.

Various other tenants and owners come and go, among them the Withall family. In 1795, in the Drake records, there appears a well-known miller, John Ebble, who during the Napoleonic wars was asked by the Parish to charge a low price for his flour as the villagers were impoverished. During the Revolutionary and Napoleonic wars over some twenty years, the Parish undertook several times to provide food at less than cost price, especially flour in bulk to the poor.[13]

By 1801, M. Lee and R. Snow have taken over from Mr. Ebble, and in 1804, there is a lease for 21 years from R. Snow to the well-known Linscott family, who were the millers until the 1920s. William Linscott built The Firs *(see Chapter III)* as his retirement home in 1902, when he handed over the running of the Mill to his nephew, Edwin. A subsequent miller, William Harrison Mallet, was a direct descendent of John Harrison the great eighteenth century clockmaker who invented the marine chronometer, which enabled sailors to find the longitude of their position.

It continued as a working mill up to the 1950s, when a retired eye-surgeon, Dr. Flint, bought it as a home, which it has remained.

---

[1] Primitive Methodism was a major movement in the English Methodism from about 1810 to the Methodist Union in 1932. The Primitives were evangelical revivalists, and their hymns were sung to popular tunes. Their preachers were plainly dressed and poorly paid, and they encouraged the young, the poor and women to preach. By 1883 when Lympstone Chapel was built, they had become much more conservative, and were on their way to reconciliation with the Wesleyans.

[2] The chapel was deconsecrated and sold in 2009 and has become the band room for the Lympstone South-West Telecoms Band.

3 This building is now the Methodist Church, and is also used as a hall.

4 Tenements were favourite descriptions in the eighteenth/nineteenth centuries in indentures or conveyances.

5 His Will of 1822 gave most of his property to his son, William Bass, but alternatively specified others of his family if William had no heirs. He also bequeathed "all those four dwellinghouses in Lympston called the 'Bridge Houses' to his daughter, Eliza Coleridge Sivell." In the event, it was Eliza who came into it all. It was also put forcibly that her legacy was to be "free from the debts and engagements of her Husband…"

6 William Bass Sivell, son of Eliza Coleridge Sivell, originally of Esher, Surrey, was described as "Architect" or "Gentleman". He was almost certainly the designer of Peters Tower (q.v.).

7 Otherwise known as Mitherills, Metherals, etc.

8 This 'modernisation' was common in Lympstone. At least four houses here adopted Georgian fenestration, porticos, columns and details for the façade.

9 Captain Metheral in his Will of 1727 set up a charity for the poor children of Lympstone, through an annuity of £4 from his premises, "a messuage garden orchard and two fields thereto adjoining … the …dwellinghouse, and two other tenements situate at Lympstone Strand". This was for their education, "until they were able to read the Bible", and was to continue always (John Bass did continue it), but at some time before 1858 the charity lapsed.

10 This is called Quarry Field in the 1839 Tithe Map of Lympstone.

11 Being "in mercy" meant a fine was handed down by the Court, manorial or other.

12 As the richest heiress in England, Cecily was naturally married off to the King's stepson, the Marquis of Dorset.

13 These notes are in the Parish Records of 1795: "John Ebble's bill for the grinding of wheat and barley being now produced, and it appearing he hath detained to his own use 42 bushels of the dressing of the barley supposed to be worth six pence a bushel, William Elliot is ordered to debit the amount thereof, being £1.1s.0d. out of the amount of Mr. Ebble's bill being £4.1s.4d…"

Chapter X

Along the A376 and down Strawberry Hill

We now start again from the A376, from Exmouth to Exeter. On the west side of the main road lies a group of small terrace houses known as **Jubilee Grove**. From the 1930s there was a shop here, the Jubilee Stores. Further on nos. **1-5 Haynes Cottages** originally formed part of a single large medieval farmhouse, now divided into two houses, Crooks' Corner and Olde Hollow.

Crooks Corner and Olde Hollow

Crooks' Corner has a reserved air and does not show its secrets easily. From the road, you see only the gable end. The farmhouse dates from the fifteenth or early sixteenth century, and is built of roughcast cob and sandstone rubble. It now has a pantile roof, just one of innumerable additions and alterations. In the late eighteenth century the main house was extended at both ends and a cross wing built on the service end. In the nineteenth century there were more extensions, and in 1949 a rear wing was built. This was probably carried out by the same owner who is said to have introduced many old beams, brought in from elsewhere.

The house, however, retains some of its original medieval features. Of the three rooms, the hall and the service end were open to the roof, with resultant smoke-blackened beams. Although the inner room was always of two storeys with a stair-turret to the rear, the first floors and the chimney stacks would not have been added until the late sixteenth or seventeenth centuries.

In the one-bay, very small hall, there is a surviving passage screen hidden behind internal rendering. There are also three chamfered ceiling beams. The stairs in the rear turret retain their medieval treads and risers hidden beneath present day carpentry.

Harefield Lodge

A pair of tall limestone gate piers stand on the other side of the main road. They once heralded the driveway to Harefield House. Behind them are two detached lodges, built in about 1830, probably by William Burgess, the architect of the house (*see Chapter I*). They are of a single storey and have barley-sugar brick shafts. There are double gates with railings, and much fancy ironwork, looking imposing as the traffic rushes by.

Thorn Farm

The plain farmhouse lies at the bottom of a hill with the farmyard to its right. Behind are rich meadows rising to Harefield House and beyond. It dates from the seventeenth century, though it may incorporate earlier work. It is a three-room, through-passage layout, common in medieval houses. Thorn Farm is mentioned in a Lay Subsidy Roll of 1330 as being owned by William atte Thorn. It has formed part of the Peters' estate since the nineteenth century, and the numerous tenant farmers' names are known during that century and up to today.

We now turn left off the main road at the top of a hill by **Gulliford Burial Ground**. This was the old Dissenters' Meeting Place with (formerly) a chapel. It is enclosed in brick walls (and with a mounting block) immediately inside Meeting Lane. Eighteenth and nineteenth century gravestones lean at jaunty angles. When the wild flowers and grasses are allowed to grow, it is a romantic and evocative spot. It was once very popular for visiting, and frequented by Dissenters from the well-to-do and merchant sectors, such as the Barings, the Lees and the Smiths, who would come in their carriages.

Before this and the fork in the road, is a small drive to the right to an old cottage.

Boundary Cottage

Boundary Cottage, a cob and thatched detached dwelling by the A376, is probably of 1689. An oil painting of 1744 (conserved in the Exmouth Library) of Gulliford's second Chapel shows the cottage in the background.[1]

It was built of roughcast cob as a two- or three-room cross passage type house, with a rear wing. There was a stair turret in the angle formed by the main range and rear wing, a feature usually found in sixteenth or seventeeenth century buildings. The end stacks have been replaced, and there have been other repairs and alterations. Additions have included twentieth century casements to the ground floor and the rear wing, when the stair turret was demolished.

The first known facts about the cottage appear in an Indenture of 1880, when it was called Rowlands.[2] We learn that it was by then in two parts, with "a Courtyard and well of water there in common with the occupier of the Dwelling house adjoining…" An Exeter solicitor, Thomas Floud, owned the first part of the house, and allowed his wife to buy the cottage from him for £50, which she promptly sold to a Mr Orchard. This was perhaps a concession on his part, as the Married Women's Property

Act, whereby women were allowed to own property in their own right, did not come in until 1883. Perhaps there was some tax advantage in this arrangement.

In 1954, William Brook Hallett, a well-known local farmer, sold the cottage with planning permission for a tea garden and new entrance to the car park. It was in 1996 that substantial alterations were made, the north wall of the old cottage knocked down, and further rooms and a verandah completed.

The remaining rooms, however, have many old structural features, notably a solid beam with chamfered ends across what is now the living room, once two small rooms divided by wooden partitions.

After the drive, with a large car park above the house, we come to a fork in the road, with Meeting Lane to the right, leading to the Royal Marine quarters and the council houses, and Strawberry Hill to the left. There are many fields and trees around this spot, though the village begins to reach out on either side of the lanes very shortly.

Taking the left fork, we descend Strawberry Hill, at first surrounded by trees and fields, soon to become enclosed by houses. On the east side there are some more modern houses and then we reach **The Grange**, the first of a number of Victorian and Edwardian houses which came to be built on this hill.

The house was built of brick and is nineteenth century.[3] To Strawberry Hill it presents a façade of three gables with a riot of decorative barge boarding, an oriel window and a grandiose entrance doorway. It was first mentioned in the 1841 Census; and was called Strawberry Hill from 1850, when it was owned by Mrs Henrietta Wyatt.[4] After a later owner, Lt. Col. Thomas Birch, died, the estate was sold off in 1923. Birch Road and Grange Close were later built on the land.

Further down on the west side, an orange-painted brick entrance arch with panelled doors and kitsch winged beasts introduces us to **Lympstone House**, a large plain villa with a wing. The gardens are enclosed by limestone walls, part of which were recently well repaired on the corner of Strawberry Hill and Church Road. These walls enclose one of the finest groups of large trees in Lympstone, forming a spectacular feature of the landscape of the village. During World War I, the land belonging to Lympstone House on the opposite side of the road was used as a camp for soldiers, and traces are found round there when people dig their gardens.[5]

[1] The first Chapel was built in 1689 on ground owned and donated by a Woodbury man, Thomas Lee of Sparkshayes, whose field was then inside the Woodbury boundary (which came across the main road). A reproduction of the painting can be found on an information board inside the Gulliford Burial Ground. This chapel was demolished and a second one built in 1774 (paid for by Charles Baring of Courtlands), when the Dissenters had become Unitarians. Eventually at the turn of the nineteenth/twentieth century, this second chapel had to be taken down. The Chapel in Lympstone was built when people got tired of walking so far to Gulliford, and the site became a Burial Ground only.

[2] Nothing has come to light so far about the owners in the Directories or Census.

[3] In 2002 a window was uncovered in the brick during exterior renovation. There are cellars to this house.

[4] Henrietta Wyatt gave a beautiful altarpiece to the church in the 1840s, and endowed the National Schools' mistress, giving her £24 a year salary.

[5] There were English soldiers up Strawberry Hill, and American ones in camps in the Longmeadow Road fields, it is said by older inhabitants.

A Final View

Having looked at many significant houses in Lympstone, an old estuary village of about two thousand people, what have we seen?

We talked of lifting the veils of history by looking in detail at the houses. Sadly, the further back one goes, the less documentation there is, though architecture, archaeology and geology can help to overcome the lack of written information. In England in general, it is probable that a historian can trace our buildings back to the Middle Ages. After this, however, it is a matter of little certainty.

Houses first built in medieval times still exist in Lympstone, though much altered. We have observed some of the characteristics of different periods, and hope there will be more pride in preserving the ancient character of our dwellings, inside as well as out. During alterations, it should be possible to incorporate such features. Indeed, if it is a listed house, you cannot remove anything that contributes to the architectural and historic interest without first obtaining listed building consent.

Lympstone has an abundance of listed houses in the parish, which is a living community. In what form will it continue? The inhabitants have faced many changes, both climatically and economically. They have survived by adapting.. Famine and floods, bad harvests and declining fisheries, new authorities and governments, changing religions and standards, incoming inhabitants, have challenged in their turn. Through it all, however, there has been a strong community which finds a way through difficulties, and demonstrates a will to survive.

Whilst we have seen buildings of cob, stone and brick arise, the biggest enemy to our village environment today is insensitive development. Building projects and roads can change the whole character of a village. If Lympstone is to remain a special place, new building should respect its particular character. In the case of old buildings, this means that the existing proportions and materials should be observed. Lympstone derives its character from individuality and variety, and new building in the twenty first century should continue this tradition. Stock housing estates by developers are not appropriate.

In the face of uPvc doors and windows, the expansion of Exmouth, and the pressure to build more and more houses, the question that faces Lympstone in the decades and centuries to come is this:

Will a rising tide of development swallow up the village and its natural beauty, and with it an enterprising, special community?

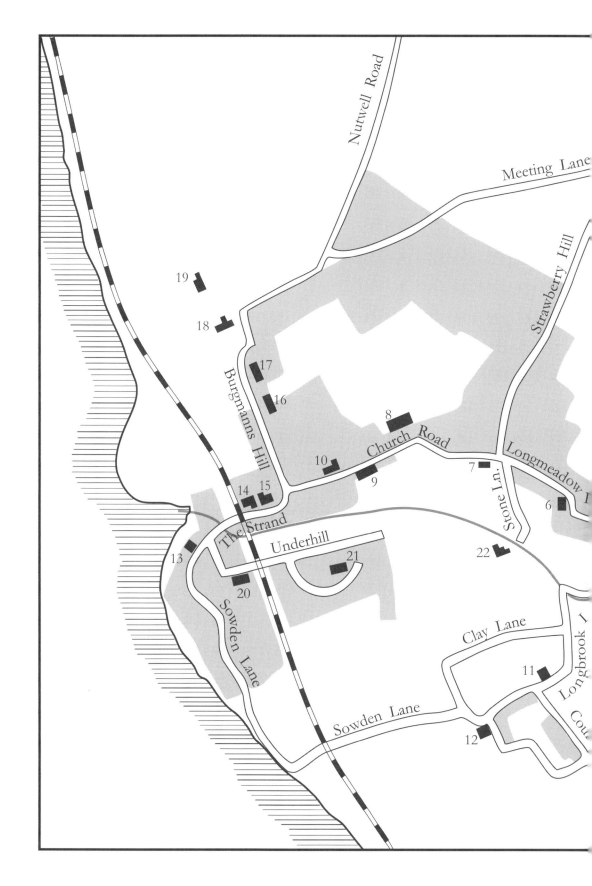

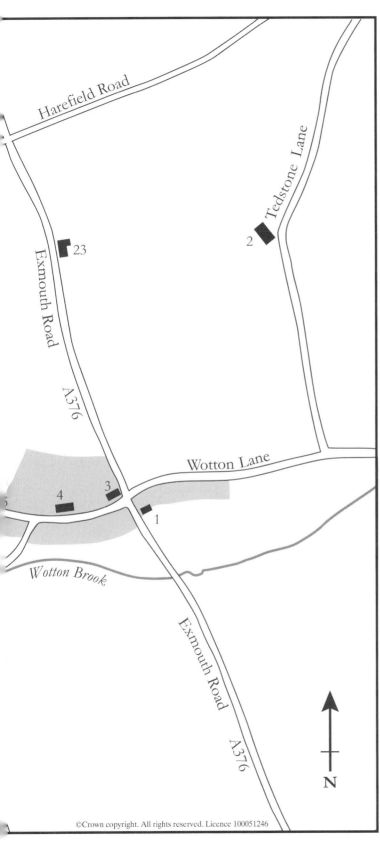

1. Bronte House
2. Harefield House (St Peter's School)
3. Vine Cottage
4. Berry Cottage
5. Rogues Roost
6. Elmside, Bass's Orchard and Lavender Cottage
7. Hares
8. Parish Church
9. Havering, Eleanors and Sheppards
10. Varnes
11. Sowden House
12. Sowden Farm
13. Limekiln House
14. Queen Anne House
15. Bridgethorpe
16. Merrylands
17. Manor House
18. Hayes Raleigh
19. Belvedere
20. Underhill House, Kilrush and Metherells
21. The Sanctuary and Sunny Bank
22. The Mill
23. Thorn Farm
24. Boundary Cottage

GLOSSARY

Bargeboarding
Projecting boards placed against the incline of the gable. Often decorated.

Brickwork
A stretcher is a brick laid lengthways, a header end on. The most common pattern is Flemish bond, where headers and stretchers alternate in each row. English bond has alternate rows of headers and stretchers, and can be seen in Lympstone on the railway bridges.

Cross-passage house

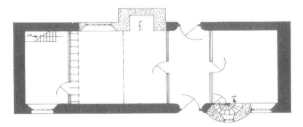

Entry is into a passage across the house, with screens to rooms either side. Originally on one side of the passage was a 'hall' or living room, often with a further inner room beyond, and on the other a service room.

Crucks
Pairs of large curved timbers used as the principals framing the structure of a house.

Fanlight
A window, often semi-circular, over a door, with radiating glazing bars.

Glebe
Cultivated land apportioned to a clergyman as part of his benefice.

Hipped roof
With sloped instead of vertical ends

Lucarne
A small opening in a spire, to let out the sound of the bells or chimes.

Pantiles
Roofing tile of curved S-shaped sections.

Pilaster
Shallow column, projecting only slightly from a wall.

Plank and muntin
A screen formed of vertical joists (muntins) with planks in between.

Sgraffito
Decoration on plaster of incised patterns.

Stucco
Slow-setting very fine plaster used as an external rendering.

Tuck pointing
Joints filled flush with mortar coloured to match the bricks, and then scored with a narrow groove into which a thin ribbon of contrasting mortar is pressed ot 'tucked'.

Windows
Lympstone has a window type not found elsewhere. It has the structure of Yorkshire lights, which are horizontal sliding windows, but in Lympstone they have the additional feature of small wooden pegs standing up from the sill. They are said to have been made by one village carpenter.

A Lympstone light in East View Cottages

In the garden of Field House